The complete paintings of

Raphael

Introduction by **Richard Cocke**

Notes and catalogue by **Pierluigi de Vecchi**

Harry N. Abrams, Inc. *Publishers* New York

**Classics of the
World's Great Art**

Editor
Paolo Lecaldano

International Advisory Board
Gian Alberto dell' Acqua
André Chastel
Douglas Cooper
Lorenz Eitner
Enrique Lafuente Ferrari
Bruno Molajoli
Carlo L. Ragghianti
Xavier de Salas
David Talbot Rice
Jacques Thuillier
Rudolf Wittkower

*This series of books is
published in Italy by Rizzoli
Editore, in France by
Flammarion, in the United
Kingdom by Weidenfeld and
Nicolson, in the United States
by Harry N. Abrams, Inc.,
in Spain by Editorial Noguer
and in Switzerland by
Kunstkreis*

Library of Congress Catalog
Card No. 69-16897
ⓒ Copyright in Italy by
Rizzoli Editore, 1966
Printed and bound in Italy

Table of contents

Photographic sources   Colour plates: Dominquez Ramos, Madrid; National Gallery, London; National Gallery of Art, Washington D.C.; Giraudon, Paris; Réunion des Musées Nationaux, Versailles; Scala, Florence;
Black and white illustrations: Alinari, Florence; Archivio Rizzoli, Milan.

Drawings and sketches by   Sergio Coradeschi

Introduction

'The greatest tragedy for painting was that Raphael died young, with a glorious reputation throughout Europe', Dolce, *Dialogo della Pittura*, 1557. Raphael's reputation as one of the greatest painters of the century was thus firmly established by the middle of the 16th century. In Dolce's dialogue Raphael's case is placed in the mouth of Aretino, who proudly claims to have been an intimate friend of Raphael in Rome. In spite of some exaggeration Dolce's dialogue must, to some extent at least, reflect Raphael's own views on painting and can serve as a useful starting point for an understanding of Raphael. Dolce bases his high assessment of Raphael on his greatness as a painter of *istoria*, on the variety of invention that Raphael shows in his painting of the nude and on his ability as a colourist.

The best English translation for *istoria* is 'history painting', and a glance at Plates XX–XXVI reveals what is involved in 'history painting'. In *The School of Athens*, for instance (Plates XX–XXI), Raphael has created a wide range of figure types, contrasting idealized young heads with those of the older philosophers. In the costumes Raphael has attempted to be historically correct, and has placed the action in an architectural setting intended to remind the spectator that this symposium is set outside of time. Plates XXIV–XXV show the skill with which Raphael has characterized the philosophers, some of whom are seated in solitary thought, whilst others use their books to teach an eager audience, and others are shown arguing. None of the gestures is repeated.

The theory of painting that lies behind this fresco, and which influenced Dolce's dialogue, was not new. It was first formulated by L.B. Alberti in his *Della Pittura* of 1435. Alberti's view that the *istoria* was the finest achievement of the painter profoundly influenced Leonardo da Vinci in his theoretical writings. Leonardo further developed the idea of decorum that was central to Alberti's view of the *istoria*. Decorum can best be explained by an example. A young man should move boldly and swiftly, in contrast with the movements of an old man. Raphael has illustrated this contrast on the left of *The School of Athens* (Plate XX), where the rushing entry of the young messenger is contrasted with the calm movement of the philosopher who shows him the way. Raphael is unlikely to have known Leonardo's theoretical writings, but he absorbed these principles by studying Leonardo's work on his arrival in Florence in 1504. Before continuing to analyse Raphael's debt to Leonardo it is best to return to Dolce's account of Raphael.

The second quality that Dolce praises – Raphael's variety of invention in painting the nude – can be illustrated by many examples, for instance, Plates XV, XXXI and LIX. In *Galatea* in the Farnesina, shown in Plate XXXIII, Raphael contrasts the firm muscular Triton with the soft graceful figure of Galathea's attendant. These figures reveal the idealization of Raphael's style, that Dolce would have taken for granted. This remains true of all Raphael's figures, from those shown in Plate IV to those in *The Sistine Madonna* (Plate LVI). Raphael himself wrote to his friend Castiglione in 1514 about the problem of painting a beautiful woman: 'I use a certain idea, which comes into my mind'. By this Raphael refers to the standard Renaissance theory that all painting should be based on idealization, not realism. This principle remained the same throughout Raphael's career, but his 'idea' of beauty changed radically from the graceful but slight figures of *The Three Graces* shown in Plate V, to the powerful and expressive figures of the Loggia di Psiche, Plate LIX.

The final virtue which Dolce attributed to Raphael was his ability as a colourist. This may seem surprising since it is now usual to contrast the 'colour' of Titian with the 'design' of Raphael. Dolce, however, coupled Raphael with Titian as great colourists, and rightly noted that Raphael's frescoes have a strength of colour that others had hardly achieved in oils. The vivid warmth of the colour in *The School of Athens* distinguishes Raphael from Leonardo, even when Raphael is most influenced by Leonardo. The brilliance of Raphael's colour, which is always linked with a precise sense of light, is further enhanced in his later frescoes. In *The Liberation of St Peter* (Plates XLV–XLVII), Raphael has painted a brilliant night scene, with beautifully observed cloud effects, and has taken special care with the vivid reflection of the torch on the armour of the captain of the guard, and has translated the appearance of the angel in terms of light, Plate XLV. The flickering, indeterminate colour and light of Plates XXXVIII and XXXIX contrasts with the calm classic light and strong colour of the Pope's Swiss Guard in another fresco in the same room shown in Plate XLI.

Dolce's analysis of Raphael's abilities as a 'history painter' applies equally to his portraiture. Raphael's portraiture has a greater range of inventiveness than that of his most outstanding rival in Rome, Sebastiano del Piombo. Raphael adopts from Leonardo's *Mona Lisa*, now in the Louvre, the massive pose of Agnolo Doni (Plate VI), which fills the panel with a triangle formed at the base by his arms. Raphael has related Doni's pose to that of his wife in the companion picture, which is similar to that shown in Plate VII, so that their two poses balance and answer one another. Raphael further extends this pose in his portraits of Baldassare Castiglione (Plate LIV), and in that of the *Donna Velata* (Plate LV). Raphael has varied their gestures and the lighting, since one is posed in a dark costume in front of a light background, whilst the creamy robes of the other are balanced against a dark background. In the portrait of Fedra Inghirami (Plate LIII), Raphael has adopted the Flemish device of showing the figure at work, so that he looks up out of the picture. As in Raphael's frescoes, the portraits give a broadly generalized account of the sitters.

Dolce's account of Raphael fails to mention both his development and the influence of Leonardo and Michelangelo on Raphael. Raphael's mastery over the nude is itself due to the influence of Michelangelo. In *The Three Virtues* (Plates XXVIII and XXIX), Raphael is struggling to absorb the first impact of the vitality and power with which Michelangelo has invested his figures on the Sistine Ceiling. By the time that Raphael created the marvellously sculptural forms shown in Plate XLII he had, as Dolce

realized, learned to rival Michelangelo's sense of form and, like Michelangelo, based his figures on a study of antiquity.

The figures in *The School of Athens* reveal Raphael's profound debt to Leonardo. The language of gesture that they use is derived from that which Leonardo had used in his panel of *The Adoration of the Magi* of 1482, and in *The Last Supper* in Sta Maria della Grazie, Milan, of 1497–8. As in Leonardo, Raphael uses gesture to heighten the narrative; a notable example is shown in Plate XL where the gestures of the spectators focus attention upon the miracle which is the subject of the fresco. This contact with artistic developments in Florence in the early part of the 16th century was vital to Raphael's development.

His early pictures show his mastery of the backward-looking idiom of his first master, Pietro Perugino (c. 1445/50–1523). Raphael's relationship with Perugino can be clearly seen in one of his most famous pictures, *The Marriage of the Virgin* of 1504, now in the Brera, Milan (Plate II). Both the composition and the individual figures are derived from Perugino's version of this theme now in the museum at Caen, which was painted at the same time as the Raphael. The narrow range of conventional expressions reveals the limitations of Perugino's style, limitations which still hamper Raphael's attempt to achieve a clear narrative, in which the figures play a distinct role. Raphael is already searching for the expressiveness of *The School of Athens*, but the means available to him remain rudimentary.

The composition of *The Marriage of the Virgin* reveals another facet of Raphael's mastery of the *istoria* – one that Dolce does not mention – his skill in relating the overall design of the panel to the shape of the frame. Raphael's early panels cannot be fully understood without their frames, which complete the composition. In *The Marriage of the Virgin* the rounded shape of the temple in the background and its dome are carefully related to the curved top of the panel. This is further echoed in the reversed curve of the figures in the foreground. Raphael reveals a similar sensitivity to the shape which he has to decorate in his later works. In *The School of Athens* the composition is derived from Leonardo's *Last Supper*, but Raphael relates it successfully to the fresco field by the curve of the barrel vault which echoes the frame of the fresco, and in the hollowed-out grouping of the philosophers which again very loosely echoes the round frame. Another notable example of

Raphael's compositional skill can be seen in his use of the tondo. In the *Madonna della Sedia* (Plate LII), for instance, Raphael has brilliantly fitted the Madonna and Child into the form of the panel by bending the Madonna's neck, and by echoing the shape of the panel in the soft roundness of her right arm. Raphael achieves a similarly sensitive solution in *The Alba Madonna* (Plate XXXVI).

Raphael's ability to fit his fresco to the site is equally important for the frescoes of the Loggia di Psiche in the Farnesina (Plate LIX). Originally the loggia opened directly into a garden. The decoration of the site was further complicated by the fact that the heavy central stemma was already in situ when Raphael began. The frescoes are not complete, as the original scheme would have included extra frescoes in the lunettes now decorated with illusionistic windows. Raphael painted the ceiling with an open framework of flowers and branches, behind which blue sky can be seen. He painted two large tapestries which appear to hang from the floral frame on which he showed the main action of the fresco, *The Feast of the Gods*. The effect makes brilliant use of the site and its relationship to the garden of the villa.

Dolce, as we have already noted, did not discuss Raphael's development. This was made possible by the achievement of Leonardo and Michelangelo, but only Raphael was able to synthesize these differing stylistic developments into a personal style. Even at the time of Raphael's death his style was still changing and progressing. No one can predict how Raphael would be developed had he lived. Europe indeed had reason to mourn his premature death.

RICHARD COCKE

An outline of the artist's critical history

We may readily endorse the critics' reservations about the authenticity of Francesco Francia's sonnet in praise of Raphael; written – if it is in fact by him – in 1511. Between 1515 and 1516, however, the artist was mentioned by Ariosto in the famous passage, quoted below, in *Orlando Furioso*, from which it is clear that Raphael, though scarcely past thirty, was already a legend. Dozens of verses, besides those quoted below, confirm the fact. Soon, in addition to impressive but critically barren flights of praise, judgments were formulated, as we see, from the works of Aretino (by way of Dolce especially), Serlio and Vasari. But although these began by granting him pre-eminence in inspiration and natural grace, facility and strict perspective, seemliness and propriety, the judgments which were hardly less critically barren soon reduced his qualities to the level of academic pedantry; and by relegating him to first among equals amounted to open confessions of a confrontation of Raphael – even on a moral plane – with the 'terrible' Buonarotti (by the Tusco-Roman mannerists) and with Titian 'the colourist' (by those of Venice). Art historians of the 17th century either echoed earlier praise yet again or put Sanzio, the Carraccis and all their school in the same class, always in the name of propriety and grace (in the more favourable cases, at least) – qualities which the 18th century found personified in Correggio.

As soon as he was caught up in neoclassic deliberations about ideal, absolute beauty, Raphael regained esteem. However, he soon lost this, since the Romantics valued his harmony less and less, convinced, as they were, that art must be torment. New arguments grew out of this in favour of his rival, in that inconceivable comparison with Michelangelo. Otherwise his appeal lay in the socio-religious edification he offered, and in this context the very term PreRaphaelitism removes the need for any further clarification. This disfavour might have continued right into our century had not Balzac, the great Romantic, captured for us the vitality that breathes through Raphael's figures and the prodigies of his style. Moreover another Romantic, Delacroix, had made almost equally important discoveries which were enlarged upon in their turn by the propounders of 'pure visibility' (Wölfflin, Dvořák, etc.) in their examination of structural order. Later critics such as Longhi, Ortolani, (but with reservations in his esteem) Briganti, Ragghianti and others, through scrutinizing the civilization of the figures in Raphael, were at last to give aesthetic consistency to the famous 'arch-painter', but in such elevated, vague terms as to be liable to the heavy intolerance usually reserved for the 'too perfect' magniloquence which still seems to mar the judgments of many a layman and some avant-garde specialists today.

. . . You alone to whom Heaven gave the fatal gift
which excels and surpasses all others,
teach us your excellent artifice
which makes you equal to the ancients. . . .
F. FRANCIA (?), *All'excellente pittore Raffaello Sanxio* c. 1511 (?)

. . . those who were once with us, or are now,
Leonardo, Andrea Mantegna, Gian Bellino,
the two Dossis, and he who both sculpts and paints,
Michel, more than mortal, an angel divine;
Bastiano, Rafael, Titian, who honours
no less Cador than they Venice and Urbino . . .
L. ARIOSTO, *Orlando Furioso*, 1515–6

. . . a young man of immense goodness and admirable intelligence.
C. CALCAGNINI, Letter of Iacob Ziegler, 1519 (?) (*Opera aliquot*, 1544)

. . . had he lived until old age, he would have been another Michelangelo.
C. DE FINE, *Ephemerides historicae* (c. 1520) (ms in the Biblioteca Vaticana, Cod. Oct. 1613 and 1614)

. . . that unique painter, whose work
made lowly each work of Nature. . .
G. CASIO, *Sonetto per Rafaele da Urbino* (book entitled *Cronica*, 1525)

. . . in so much as he is considered to have no equals in this respect (perspective), nor betters, and for the rest to be a divine painter, as I shall always call him . . .
S. SERLIO, *Regole generali di architettura*, 1537

. . . when I saw the sketch for the whole of Michelangelo's *Last Judgment* I finally understood the illustrious charm of Raphael, its pleasing beauty of invention . . .
P. ARETINO, Letter to A. Corvino, July 1547 (actually to Michelangelo, November 1545)

... you judge ... painting the most noble of the arts, when contemplating the divine paintings of that excellent artist Raphael of Urbino ...
M. A. BIONDO, *De la nobilissima pittura*, 1549

He was commended, with high and proper praise, for the vague sweet air which he, more than any other painter, was able to confer on the figures he composed.
S. FORNARI, *La Spositione . . . sopra L'Orlando Furioso di M. Ludovico Ariosto*, 1549

... a very great painter who was compared with those ancient artists whom men of letters have listed by name: and we may clearly endorse their judgment if we look at his works.
L. ALBERTI, *Descrittione di tutta Italia*, 1550

... Nature herself has often been surpassed by my paintings and has mistaken for her own that which was the fruit of my endeavours ...
M. A. MURET, *Raphaëlis Urbinatis . . . tumulus ipse loquitur* (c. 1550) (*Carmina*, I)

... I have heard (from Michelangelo) that Raphael was not endowed by Nature with this talent (painting), but achieved it through extensive study.
A. CONDIVI, *Vita di Michelagnolo Buonarroti*, 1553

... frankly, it can be said that Raphael's painting is complete and perfect ...
SABBA DA CASTIGLIONE, *Ricordi*, 1555

I know that in Rome while Raphael was alive, most of the literati and art experts considered him a better painter than Michelangelo. Those who acclaimed Michelangelo were mostly sculptors who looked no further than his draftsmanship and the 'terribilità' of his figures. They believed that Raphael's charming and graceful style was too easy and therefore not really art. They did not realize that 'facility' is the principal requirement for excellence in any art and the most difficult to achieve. It is art to hide art. Other talents all very necessary are required of the painter besides that of draftsmanship.
L. DOLCE, *Dialogo della pittura*, 1557

... take two examples of our epoch, Raphael and Michelangelo, whose paintings are resplendent with the teachings and observation of antiquity and their own skill and ability ...
F. DE GUEVARA, *Comentarios de la pintura*, 1560 (?)

Michelangelo strove ever to restore art to his own image of antiquity ... Then Raphael of Urbino ... contributed much to this art and, had he lived, we could have expected great things from him. ...
G. A. GILIO, *Due dialogi*, 1564

... Raphael of Urbino, who would have been first in painting, had it not been for Michelangelo ...
B. VARCHI, *Orazione funerale . . . nell'essequie di Michelagnolo Buonarroti*, 1564

... he enriched the art of painting with that total perfection, which can be found in the ancient statues of Apelles and Zeuxis, and more, if it be possible ... Whereupon Nature was overcome by his colours; his invention was simple and distinctive, as is apparent to anyone who observes his work ...
G. VASARI, *Le Vite*, 1568

... with skill and intelligence he has brought painting back to where it is now ...
P. VIRGILIO, *De rerum inventoribus*, 1576

... of all other painters he was exact in his use of colour, and especially in making the drapery a little darker than the flesh, giving to each, however, its own complete beauty and relief. As a draftsman, he is always accurate, composing the various parts of his figures with majesty and proportion and adorning them with the celebrated beauty of the paintings of the famous ancients. He will never be equalled nor surpassed at any time. In addition to this, he is praised and admired principally for the nobility, beauty and grace he gives to horses, as well as other animals, buildings, drapery, hair, headgear and foliage. The soft and loving light outlining his figures makes them appear beautifully vague and intricate. They are so highly modelled that they seem about to turn around with that typically Raphaelesque grace that no one else has ever been able to portray ... he is a felicitous portraitist of beautiful women ...
G. P. LOMAZZO, *Idea del Tempio della pittura*, 1590

... excellent as an architect, supreme as a painter ...
B. BALDI, *Memorie concernenti . . . Urbino*, 1590

... Full of majesty and full of dignity,
his intelligence was so great
that each work of his is worth a fortune.
Never has there been another to equal him ...
F. ZUCCARI, *Il lamento della pittura* (c. 1590), 1605

(Federico Zuccari) concluded that Raphael of Urbino was endowed through study and through Nature with all the grace and beauty to be found in art. He was the true master and imitator of all the grace and beauty contained in Nature and art in every respect ...
R. ALBERTI, *Origine et progresso dell'Accademia . . . di Roma* (1599), 1604

... from his study of antiquities Raphael was able to form his Idea of beauty, a beauty which cannot be found in Nature.
L. GRIGNAN (from concepts of G. B. Agucchi), *Diverse figure . . . da Annibale Carracci intagliate . . .*, 1646

I do not like Raphael at all ... Titian is by far the most illustrious.
M. BOSCHINI, *La carta del navegar pitoresco*, 1660

... his ability to draw the nude form was not as great as Michelangelo's, but his draftsmanship was purer and better. He did not paint as well or as thoroughly or as gracefully as Correggio, nor did he display as much contrast of chiaroscuro and colour as Titian, but he was far superior in composition to either Titian, Correggio, Michelangelo or any other painter who came after. His treatment of poses, heads, details, draperies, his manner of drawing, his variations, contrasts and expressions were quite beautiful, but above all else, he was favoured by the Graces to such an extent, that we can find no other painter to approach him.

C. A. DUFRESNOY, *De arte graphica* (c. 1660)

Raphael displayed precision in design, skill in composition, taste, grace, an exquisite sense of decoration, a harmonious disposition of figures according to the rules of perspective . . .: though he lacks the beautiful colour of the Lombards, they, in turn, lack his sense of proportions, design and taste. We have proof that Poussin, the greatest and most intelligent painter who ever lived, ceased to imitate Titian after a time and turned to Raphael, thereby demonstrating that he considered Raphael the finest of all painters.

G. L. BERNINI (from P. FRÉART DE CHANTELOU, *Journal de voyage du Chevalier Bernin en France*, 1665)

. . . a disciple of Nature's beauty and her great ideas . . . which Plato says is the most perfect prototype of beautiful things.

A. FÉLIBIEN, *Entretiens sur les Vies et les Ouvrages des plus excellents Peintres Anciens et Modernes*, 1666

. . . if one is not well informed on this particular style (of historical coherence and geometric perfection) in Italy and especially in Lombardy and Venice, it is very surprising to see the works of the great painters such as Titian, Giorgione, Tintoretto, Veronese, Palma, Bassano and others, excellent colourists and gifted in the composition of figures. The works of the great Raphael and others of the same school, however, produce a different effect on us. They gradually take possession of our soul and leave such an impression that the more we look at them the more satisfied we are, because we are continually discovering new qualities.

A. BOSSE, *Le peintre converty aux précises et universelles règles de son art*, 1667

He raised his art in its ultimate features to the height of its beauty, restoring it to its ancient mobility, and enriching it with all the graces and gifts which had rendered it glorious among the Greeks and Romans.

G. P. BELLORI, *Le vite de' pittori, scultori et architetti moderni*, 1672

. . . Those historical scenes and beautiful paintings in the Vatican (Stanze) that enrapture whoever views them, should be the object of continual praise, both written and spoken, from men of learning. Let their fame spread from one Pole to the other.

L. SCARAMUCCIA, *Le Finezze de' pennelli italiani*, 1674

. . . he taught a world without light about composition and narrative painting . . .

C. C. MALVASIA (from concepts of F. Albani, c. 1630), *Felsina pittrice*, 1678

The essence of painting consists in the imitation of 'visible objects' and in this respect Raphael and the Roman school are

worth no more than mediocre consideration.

R. DE PILES, *Dissertations sur les ouvrages des plus fameux peintres comparés avec ceux de Rubens*, 1681

. . . he was unsurpassed in every respect and seems to embody all the good qualities of the ancients.

G. P. BELLORI, *Descrizione delle immagini dipinte da Raffaello nelle camere del Palazzo . . . Vaticano*, 1695

. . . so many of his beautiful works suffer from a lack of colour which would attract the admiration of the curious.

R. DE PILES, *Cours de peinture par principes*, 1708

See how he has chosen the most perfect human forms and created a perfect union of their members through the harmonious diversity of parts. Admire the solidity, the force and the relief of these figures which never lose their tenderness, grace or sprightliness. See how he has attuned the disagreeable with the agreeable, the severe with the soft, the jovial with the sombre. Examine the bizarreness of ideas, the judicious style of composition, the appropriate contrasts, the elegance of the characters, the abundance of concepts, the fertility of invention. Observe how excellently he has judged the distance of grounds, the arrangement of the setting, the position and diminution of objects, and the understanding of light and shadow. And mark that no one better than he knows how to express with a brush the actions of the body and the passions of the soul.

L. PASCOLI (from concepts of C. Maratta), *Vite de' pittori, scultori ed architetti moderni*, 1730

Only in Raphael, Guido Reni and Annibale Carracci can all the qualities of the perfect painter be found.

H. WALPOLE, *Aedes Walpolianae*, 1747

His genius, however, formed to blaze and to shine might, like fire in combustible matter, for ever have lain dormant, if it had not caught a spark by its contact with Michel Angelo: and though it never burst out with extraordinary heat and vehemence, yet it must be acknowledged to be a more pure, regular, and chaste flame. Though our judgement must upon the whole decide in favour of Raffaele, yet he never takes such a firm hold and entire possession of the mind as to make us desire nothing else, and to feel nothing wanting.

J. REYNOLDS, *Discourses on Art* (*Discourse five, delivered to the Students of the Royal Academy, on the Distribution of the Prizes, December 10, 1772*)

If we judge him for beauty alone, Raphael is incontestably the most eminent. He is, however, second to Titian and Correggio in colour and chiaroscuro . . . As a draftsman, Raphael is admirable for his proportions and movements, and the expression of grace, elegance, suitability, nobility and simplicity. But with regard to form, he copied individual beauty as he found it and in this fashion never understood Nature's beauty. . . .

F. MILIZIA, *Dell' arte di vedere nelle belle arti*, 1781

. . . The reason why not everyone likes Raphael's works at first sight is because their beauty is intellectual and not visual. Thus, beauty is not perceived immediately, but only after it has

penetrated the intellect . . .
A. R. MENGS, *Opere*, 1783

Raphael always succeeded in doing what others longed to do.
W. GOETHE, *Italienische Reise*, 1786

A natural tendency for selecting what is beautiful, an intellectual gift for extracting one perfect example of beauty from many different examples, a very lively spirit, and a delight in representing the formal aspects of a momentary impassioned act; a facility of brushwork put in the service of concepts of the imagination. Only Nature could have given him these gifts . . .
L. LANZI, *Storia pittorica della Italia*, 1795

Maximum clarity and at the same time maximum mobility and profundity: this is the incomparable character of the works of Raphael, which, though they do not in many ways resemble external appearances, can be compared to the paintings of the ancients.
V. KOLLOF, *Beschreibung der Museen zu Paris*, 1811

. . . no one has made such advances in the science of drawing as Michelangelo; in the natural use of colour, as Titian; in the enchantment of brush strokes and chiaroscuro, as Correggio; in invention and composition, as Raphael. But when we compare these four great painters, it cannot be denied that Raphael alone has approached each of his three rivals in that which we may call their exclusive accomplishments; whereas no one of them has equalled Raphael in the qualities in which he excels. Herein lies his incontestable pre-eminence.
QUATRMÈRE DE QUINCY, *Histoire de la vie et des ouvrages de Raphael* (1824), 1835[3]

Like true Parisians, accustomed to the highly animated expressions of our modern painters who aim at popular acclaim . . . most of Raphael's heads seem cold to us. After eight months in Rome, we begin to be cured of our bad taste . . .
STENDHAL, *Promenades dans Rome*, 1829

He has none of the somewhat theatrical dignity of Poussin, which always appears forced on the part of the artist in order to maintain a tone that is not really his own. He does not have the studied and sometimes affected grace of Leonardo. There is no other example of his genre of elegance. A sort of chaste fantasy, the terrestrial manifestation of a soul conversant with the gods. He has neither the pomp, nor the grandiose ideas, nor the sometimes indiscreet profusions of the Venetian painters. Both his simplest compositions, and those immense and majestic works vibrant with life and movement, are equally diffused with the most absolute order and an echanting harmony.

He is never banal. One never finds in his work those figures which some artist ironically called figures 'for hire' – that type of insipid 'filler' common to so many paintings. He is never too scrupulous about the refinement of every single detail; such preoccupations are more often than not accompanied by a total lack of expression.

His sole desire is that nothing should be cold and useless, that nothing could be removed at will and applied elsewhere.
E. DELACROIX, in *Revue de Paris*, 1830

Form is like Proteus, but far more difficult to grasp and far more astute. Only after a long struggle can it be forced to show itself in its true aspect. As for you, you are satisfied with the first appearance offered you, or at most, the second or third. But not so the great artists. They did not let themselves be deceived by such subterfuge, but persevered until Nature revealed herself in her true spirit. Such is the manner of Raphael . . . his immense superiority stems from the intimate impression of his desire to conquer Form. We perceive Form in his work as a means of transmitting ideas and sensations – a vast poem. Each figure is a world, a portrait taken from a sublime vision drenched in light, selected by an inner voice, traced by a celestial finger which, in the passing of a lifetime, reveals the sources of expression. You manufacture for your women beautiful garments of flesh, fine draperies of hair, but where is the blood which generates calm or passion and all the other particular effects? . . . Your figures are faintly coloured ghosts parading before us and you call them painting and art. Then, because you have fashioned something that looks more like a woman than a house, you think you have achieved your purpose . . . and consider yourselves stupendous artists. . . . Of course, a woman holds her head and wears her skirt thus, her eyes soften and melt with that air of resigned sweetness, the palpitating shadow of her lashes brushes her cheeks in just that fashion. And yet it is not like that. What is missing! A mere trifle and yet that trifle is everything. You offer the appearance of life without expressing that additional something which is perhaps the soul, dimly flickering over the enclosing flesh; in short, that flower of life which Titian and Raphael have captured.
H. DE BALZAC, *Le chef d'oeuvre inconnu*, 1832

Whenever a painter sets out to challenge and conquer the problems of art for his own glory, we believe that he has preferred self-love to prescribed goals. We admire the most difficult aspects of Raphael's late works and in this respect we prefer them to his early works. But we are more affected by the modest and effective simplicity of *The Disputà*, which lacks no trick of artifice, despite all our avowals that Raphael's artifice is never excessive.
A. BIANCHINI, *Del purismo nelle arti*, c. 1836

He succeeded in unifying the most elevated sentiments, in conformity with the requirements of the Church and the religious mission of art, with a thorough knowledge and loving reverence of natural appearances in all their vivacity of forms and colours, and with an enlightened sense of antiquity. Nevertheless his great admiration for the ideal beauty of antiquity did not lead him to slavish imitations of the forms created by Greek sculptors whose perfection can never be equalled. He was content to be inspired in a general way by the principle of unrestricted beauty, the origin of those beautiful forms. He interpreted them in his own fashion with profundity of expression, serene clarity and talented application, previously unknown in Italy. Raphael's mastery is particularly revealed in the harmonious combination of all these elements, achieving that nobility with which we are familiar.
G. W. F. HEGEL, *Vorlesungen über die Aesthetik*, 1836–8

Pure though he may be, Raphael is but a material spirit in

unabated search of the tangible, but that rogue Rembrandt is a powerful idealist who sets us dreaming and divining far beyond.
C. BAUDELAIRE, *Oeuvres*, 1846

The most conscientious of artists, he was never satisfied with the technical results of what he had done. But if one requires of him the glowing colour of Titian and the chiaroscuro of Correggio, this shows an entire misunderstanding of his true value. None of his pictures would gain essentially by the addition of these qualities, because none depended on them for their success.
J. BURCKHARDT, *Der Cicerone*, 1855

He is never carried away by his subject. He remains sober and moderate, avoiding extremes of movement and expression, purifying his models and adapting their poses. He is endowed with a natural talent for moderation, an affectionate instinct, a moral and physical delicacy which in every instance prompts him to choose the most noble and gentle creatures and all that is felicitous, generous and deserving of tenderness. His exceptional good fortune in living at a moment of culmination in art separating the achievements of the preparatory phase from the period of decadence, the singular advantage he enjoyed of a dual education in Christian innocence and purity and in Pagan vigour and joy – all these gifts and circumstances were necessary to bring him to the very top.
H. TAINE, *Voyage en Italie*, 1866

The School of Athens and the three companion paintings, illustrating the historical development of theology, poetry, and jurisprudence, constitute a celebration of culture equal in scope to Dante's Paradise and Limbo combined.
F. DE SANCTIS, *Storia della letteratura italiana*, 1870

Raphael's work unites the highest moral qualities and the marvels of technique. His painting contains something more than the beauty of forms, which have been called divine, and the magic of colour: a pervasive glow of exquisite tenderness, serene and profound faith in humanity, love of the pure, the great, and the noble . . . In the midst of general corruption, Raphael maintains a serenity that is never belied. He believes in good and beauty and tries to make his contemporaries share his convictions. Thus his work is like an ever-present stimulus to virtue. What a contrast! On the one hand, all the vices; on the other, the glorification of everything noble in man: justice, liberty, knowledge. In this respect Raphael appears to be a worthy disciple of the Greeks. He frees himself from contingent interests and passions, dominates the storm and builds on the rocks, of which Lucretius speaks, this unfettered dwelling which the tides cannot reach and which will provide an eternal refuge for humanity.
E. MÜNTZ, *Raphaël, sa vie, son oeuvre et son temps*, 1881

I went to see that painting (*Madonna of the Chair* in Florence) to pass the time and I found myself standing before a work of such freedom and stability, of such marvellous simplicity and life as one could ever imagine.
P.–A. RENOIR, *Correspondence* (1881–2)

Raphael's art represents the very best example of individualism.

His grasp of reality and Nature is as bold as is compatible with an idealistic style. Raphael is unsurpassed in just this respect. He is the most animated, the most intimate of all idealistic painters. We must therefore protest against the conventional concept of Raphael as a sugary immature artist, an idea nourished by bad, modern reproductions, classicalizing and sentimental. Raphael is of sound lineage, master of himself.
R. VISCHER, *Studien für Kunstgeschichte*, 1886

The forms in *The Disputà* are noble in intention, as they always are in Raphael's best work. But think away the spaciousness of their surroundings. What has become of the solemn dignity, the glory that radiated from them? It has gone like divinity from a god. And the other fresco, *The School of Athens*, would suffer still more from such treatment. . . .
But there is in our civilization another element which, though it is certainly much less important in our conscious intellectual life, and of much less interest to the pictorial imagination, is said, nevertheless, to be morally superior and poetically grander – all the Hebraic element, I mean, that has come to us from the Old and New Testaments . . . Raphael has brought about the extraordinary result that, when we read even the Hebrew classics, we read them with an accompaniment of Hellenic imagery. What a power he has been in modern culture, Hellenizing the only force that could have thwarted it!
B. BERENSON, *The Italian Painters of the Renaissance*, 1897

. . . The public today is accustomed to look elsewhere for the values of painting: in the facial expressions, in the spiritual interrelationships, shall we say between the subjects. Only very few realize that the essential value of these paintings does not lie in the detail but in the harmonious fusion of the groups and the all-embracing rhythm. These are decorative creations of a very high order. Decorative is used in the sense of figurations whose essential value is not contained in an isolated head or in a psychological connection, but in the placement of the images in space and their inter-reaction. Raphael understood better than any other artist before him what is pleasing to the human eye.
H. WÖLFFLIN, *Die klassische Kunst*, 1898

. . . We see (in his compositions) many beautiful, harmonious motifs, linked together either by an apparent or hidden symmetry, or by contrast.
M. DVOŘÁK, *Geschichte der italienischen Kunst* (1918–21), 1927–8

. . . since he is far more frankly and vulgarly sentimental (than Fra Bartolommeo della Porta), Raphael tends to appear more superficial and – without exaggerating – at times even silly.
R. FRY, *Transformations*, 1926

Raphael's ideal consists in a moral equilibrium, calm and serene, which completely ignores passion . . . whereas Michelangelo's ideal is one of firmness and energy, using tetragonal forms and an intimate, controlled sense of movement unlike Raphael's unconstrained and lucid flow of curves.
M. MARANGONI, *Saper vedere*, 1933

When the mythological Daphne is transformed into a laurel tree, she must pass from one world to another. We can observe a more subtle and no less singular metamorphosis, with regard to the body of a beautiful woman, from the Orléans *Madonna* to the *Madonna of the Chair*, that magnificent composition of such purity and harmony. But the most brilliant examples of Raphael's power of harmonious variation are to be found in those compositions where human figures are disposed in flowing patterns. The figures combine and recombine continually and the life of the forms has no other purpose beyond its own existence and its own renewal. The scholars of *The School of Athens* . . . the fishermen of *The Miraculous Draught of Fishes*, Imperia seated at the feet of Apollo, kneeling before Christ, are the successive elaborations of a formal concept that has as its base the human body which it uses in an interplay of symmetries, contrasts and alternations. In the metamorphosis of the figures the contribution of reality is not rejected, but a new life is created, no less complex than that of the grotesque figures of Romanesque art and of Asian mythology.

H. FOCILLON, *Vie des formes*, 1934

The artistic ideas formed in Rome, during the supreme decade from 1510 to 1520, by Raphael and his circle . . . There was that deeply considered blending first of various Italian idioms, then of Latin with Italian, of nature with history, which sometimes appears to the simple-minded like a facile compromise. It was, on the contrary, the very height of taste and genius in comparison with which the Florentines were to decline from universal significance and become provincial like Andrea del Sarto; or by a dramatic salvation were to hurl themselves like Michelangelo into the battle about Titanism and the world seen as 'torsos'. . . .

There was a cultivate ease and a method – that we might even call leopardian – of handling both the form prefigured by centuries and illustrious speech in such a way that art itself is concealed, submerged in historical understanding: it seems only a matter of dignity of manners, a life lived in calm submission to circumstances . . .

There was a rhythmic unity which moves in the very depths and enfolds all subservient nature like a royal mantle: the melodic strength which becomes harmonic rhythm, a chorus of consonance between man and things, between feeling and intellect.

R. LONGHI, *Ampliamenti dell' Officina ferrarese*, 1940

'Cathartic new' in the humanity of poetry: liberator of the drama of history.

If anyone stops to consider how and to what extent this drama influenced Italy under Julius II he will be amazed, yet not amazed, at this divine, perfect, truly final ecstasy. It gives that apogee – perched on the verge of ruin – its unreal tone, its olympic dithyramb. And anyone who wants to understand Raphael's part in the great harmonious embrace of the humanist tradition will be tempted to call him, in soul-stirred recognition, the poet of civilization, the least unhappy, perhaps, of formulae. That tradition, that civilization were the incessant leaven, motive and reason for his song. By carrying every current mode of speech, every particularity of style to their furthest limits of maturity and crystallization, in a manner not formalistically abstract but dictated by the personality of its content and even by its own 'way of life', he made them commensurate with himself, sharpened them on his whetstone, and

thus pervaded and exhausted them. Soon they were to become 'formula' and 'literature.'

S. ORTOLANI, *Raffaello*, 1942

Let us look at the late works by Raphael and his collaborators. Form is carried to the highest degree of simplification of feeling, both in its certain, yet free, naturalness and its calm enumeration of things. Compositional balance is at once achieved with such sureness, by means of an utterly simple, natural resolution of its problems, that the results almost savour of the impersonal manifestations of an anonymous genius without any history. But through this calm depiction of a pre-ordered world there shines a divine intellectual clarity. This seems the ultimate wonderful achievement of the recollection in time of culture's long development and it evinces an immutable figurative essence, and a secure internal heritage. This culture, moreover, is so sure of itself, so much the master of its own means, that it excludes every cultural drama; and without concerning itself curiously in the long unfolding, consciously feels itself to be the last term in that development. It knows that the fulness of its presence lives within itself and therefore achieves the greatest simplicity, approaching at times the very limits of possibility and, by the secondary role recognized in execution, its own absolute extreme; the immediacy of popular art directed by tradition. Things are represented in the most obvious function of their real life, with a thoughtful calm that speaks a perfect accord of intention with the means of expression between which there is absolutely no intermediate movement.

G. BRIGANTI, *Il Manierismo e Pellegrino Tibaldi*, 1945

Raphael's greatest paintings seem so effortless that one does not usually connect them with the ideas of hard and relentless work. To many he is simply the painter of sweet Madonnas which have become so well known as hardly to be appreciated as paintings any more. For Raphael's vision of the Holy Virgin has been adopted by subsequent generations in the same way as Michelangelo's conception of God the Father. We see cheap reproductions of these works in humble rooms, and we are apt to conclude that paintings with such a general appeal must surely be a little 'obvious'. In fact, their apparent simplicity is the fruit of deep thought, careful planning and immense artistic wisdom.

E. H. GOMBRICH, *The Story of Art*, 1950

It must be agreed that nobody ever – except Masaccio – achieved such an extraordinary development in so short a time. The gentle, virginal dreamer . . . very soon expressed himself in tones of quiet poetry which became more virile, more heroic and in the end choral. The metamorphosis was able to show itself through his innate genius for translating every external element into his own language . . . for reaching unifying results even from heterogeneous and sometimes contradictory premises. In his highest conceptions he relives the life of Roman plastic art, and forms the extraordinarily perfect expression of noble feeling matured in him by natural processes, there springs that profound extension of forms in an apparent structural monotony which is neither sterile immobility, nor facile illustrative expendiency or fruit of surprising eclecticism. The very impossibility of defining these achievements within any comprehensive formula (such as might have spread Raphael's fame the quicker) is a proof of this. This expressive style denies any suggestion whatever of subject and the fundamentally romantic ideals of a misunderstood originality, but renders more intense the poetic import (even if many cannot see it): it neglects all simple geometric ordinances conveniently agreed and counterposed, but expressed solemn feeling in its composition of space and perspective. Its arrangement chastises every sensual impulse, but vibrates with intimate, positive travail. In short, when every impetuosity of schematization had been exhausted, Raphael's intellect calmly and nobly came to rest in the perished world of 'latinity', recasing in it the ample afflatus of his typical dignity and revealing it with deliberate coherence in his inextinguishable choice.

E. CAMESASCA, *Tutta la pittura di Raffaello*, I, 1956

This organizing power which lets nothing be inert or useless, knows of no contrast that may be irremediable, and tends to cancel every opposition between sense and intellect, or earth and heaven . . . Raphael's greatest fascination has lain in the perfection of his drawing in the expression of moral values . . . in the mature works indeed these pulsate an extraordinary width of sympathy for the various attitudes of human feeling. And that allows him to be a portraitist without equal . . .

A. CHASTEL, *Art et Humanisme à Florence au temps de Laurent le Magnifique*, 1959

It is ascertainable through historical inspection that such a classical style as is in the Tapestry Cartoons is the ultimate level of classicism in the High Renaissance. Except by Michelangelo, the plateau this stage of style represents is no longer inhabitable, and Raphael's tenancy of it is relatively brief. Since this high classicism is an apparent ultimate, it is not susceptible of further development in this same sense. Any measurable progressive sequel could be only toward a region of ideality so high as to verge upon abstractness, and thus upon another, and no longer substantially classical, style. At the same time, no style, this ultimate still less than others, is self-repetitively imitable by an artist of Raphael's continuously searching

temper. The very fact of this achievement of a seeming apogee of classicism posed, for Raphael, the critical problem of the subsequent direction, or re-direction of his style.

S. J. FREEDBERG, *Painting of the High Renaissance in Rome and Florence*, (1961)

The raising of Leo X to the pontifical throne changed the whole tone of the papal court. A pleasure-loving Humanist and patron of the arts, Leo X surrounded himself with men of letters, favoured the researches into antiquity and sponsored the diffusion of a culture based on Latin civilization, well understanding how much the prestige of ancient Rome would help to raise the prestige of papal Rome. This was the moment when men of letters concerned themselves with linguistic matters and attempted to enrich the vernacular by the introduction of Latin elements in order to arrive at a unified Italian idiom. They also wrote Latin poetry and set out to imitate classical comedy and revive the ancient drama. Raphael's art is remarkably synchronous with this cultural movement. His incomparably open mind absorbed its terms, and he used them with the greatest mastery. Raphael has been mentioned in connection with eclecticism, but this judgment does not take into account his remarkable critical intelligence and his exhaustive study of the major artists and schools of his own time. In fact, while the men of letters discussed the vernacular, he, with a far deeper insight into the future, made use of his rich artistic experiences in Urbino, Florence, Venice and Rome to create a new artistic language which in the span of a decade became truly Italian and gave a new direction to the course of Italian and European art.

A. M. BRIZIO, from the *Enciclopedia universale dell' arte* XI, 1966

In the eleven Roman years before his early death in 1520 Raphael did, of course, produce many works that are so dynamic, expressive and realistic that they are irrelevant of our subject; but then interspersed among them, and increasing in importance, are others that are incipiently Mannerist.

JOHN SHEARMAN, *Mannerism* (1967)

The paintings in colour

List of plates

The identification of certain characters – as, for example, in plates XXIV, XXV and XXVI – is doubtful, and reference should be made to the catalogue under 85 J and K.

In the captions to the plates the actual width of the original or of the section of the work illustrated is given in centimetres.

PLATE I   ST SEBASTIAN   Bergamo, Accademia Carrara
Whole (34 cm.)

PLATE II   THE MARRIAGE OF THE VIRGIN Milan, Brera
Whole (117 cm.)

PLATE III   MADONNA AND CHILD (MADONNA DEL GRANDUCA) Florence, Pitti
Whole (55 cm.)

PLATE IV VISION OF A KNIGHT London, National Gallery
Whole (17 cm.)

PLATE V THE THREE GRACES Chantilly, Musée Condé
Whole (17 cm.)

PLATE VI   PORTRAIT OF AGNOLO DONI Florence, Pitti
Whole (45 cm.)

PLATE VII   PORTRAIT OF A YOUNG WOMAN (LADY WITH A UNICORN) Rome, Galleria Borghese
Whole (51 cm.)

PLATES VIII-IX   THE ENTOMBMENT OF CHRIST (BORGHESE DEPOSITION) Rome, Galleria Borghese
Whole (176 cm.) and details (14.3 cm.)

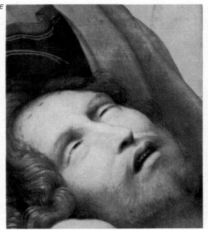

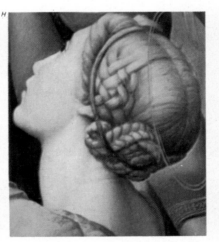

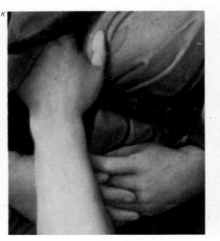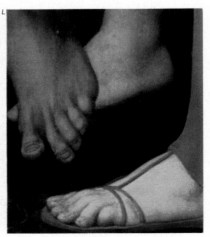

PLATE X   THE THEOLOGICAL VIRTUES (BORGHESE DEPOSITION) Rome, Pinacoteca Vaticana
Three panels, each 44 cm.

PLATE XI THE HOLY FAMILY WITH ST ELIZABETH AND THE INFANT ST JOHN (THE CANIGIANI HOLY FAMILY) Munich, Alte Pinakothek
Whole (98 cm.)

PLATE XII   MADONNA AND CHILD WITH THE INFANT ST JOHN (MADONNA OF THE GOLDFINCH) Florence, Uffizi
Whole (77 cm.)

PLATE XIII   MADONNA AND CHILD WITH THE INFANT ST JOHN (LA BELLE JARDINIÈRE) Paris, Louvre
Whole (80 cm.)

PLATE XIV   HOLY FAMILY WITH THE LAMB Madrid, Prado
Whole (21 cm.)

PLATE XV   STANZA DELLA SEGNATURA Vatican
Detail of the ceiling: *Adam and Eve* (170 cm.)

PLATE XVI STANZA DELLA SEGNATURA Vatican
Detail of *The Disputà* (225 cm.)

PLATE XVII   STANZA DELLA SEGNATURA Vatican
Detail of *The Disputà* (57 cm.)

PLATE XVIII STANZA DELLA SEGNATURA Vatican
Detail of *The Disputà* (57 cm.)

PLATE XIX STANZA DELLA SEGNATURA Vatican
Details of *The Disputà* (each 49 cm.)

PLATES XX-XXI   STANZA DELLA SEGNATURA Vatican
The School of Athens Whole (770 cm.)

PLATE XXII STANZA DELLA SEGNATURA Vatican
Detail of *The School of Athens* (308 cm.)

PLATE XXIII   STANZA DELLA SEGNATURA Vatican
Detail of *The School of Athens* (127 cm.)

PLATE XXIV STANZA DELLA SEGNATURA Vatican
Details of *The School of Athens* (each 49 cm.)

PLATE XXV STANZA DELLA SEGNATURA Vatican
Details of *The School of Athens* (small details: 49 cm.; large detail: 104 cm.)

PLATE XXVI   STANZA DELLA SEGNATURA Vatican
Details of *Parnassus* (each 92 cm.)

PLATE XXVII   STANZA DELLA SEGNATURA Vatican
Detail of *Parnassus* (157 cm.)

PLATES XXVIII-XXIX   STANZA DELLA SEGNATURA Vatican
Whole (660 cm.); details (each 130 cm.) of *The Virtues*

PLATE XXX   STANZA DELLA SEGNATURA Vatican
The Virtues (67 cm.)

PLATE XXXI   GALATEA Rome, Farnesina
Whole (225 cm.)

PLATE XXXII   GALATEA Rome, Farnesina
Detail (146 cm.)

PLATE XXXIII   GALATEA   Rome, Farnesina
Detail (106 cm.)

PLATE XXXIV   PORTRAIT OF A WOMAN (LA MUTA)   Urbino, Galleria Nazionale
Whole (48 cm.)

PLATE XXXV   PORTRAIT OF A CARDINAL Madrid, Prado
Whole (62 cm.)

PLATE XXXVI   MADONNA AND CHILD AND THE INFANT ST JOHN (THE ALBA MADONNA)   Washington, D.C.   National Gallery
Whole (diam. 98 cm.)

PLATE XXXVII   THE MADONNA OF FOLIGNO   Rome, Pinacoteca Vaticana
Detail (33 cm.)

PLATE XXXVIII   STANZA DI ELIODORO Vatican
Detail of *The Expulsion of Heliodorus from the Temple* (130 cm.)

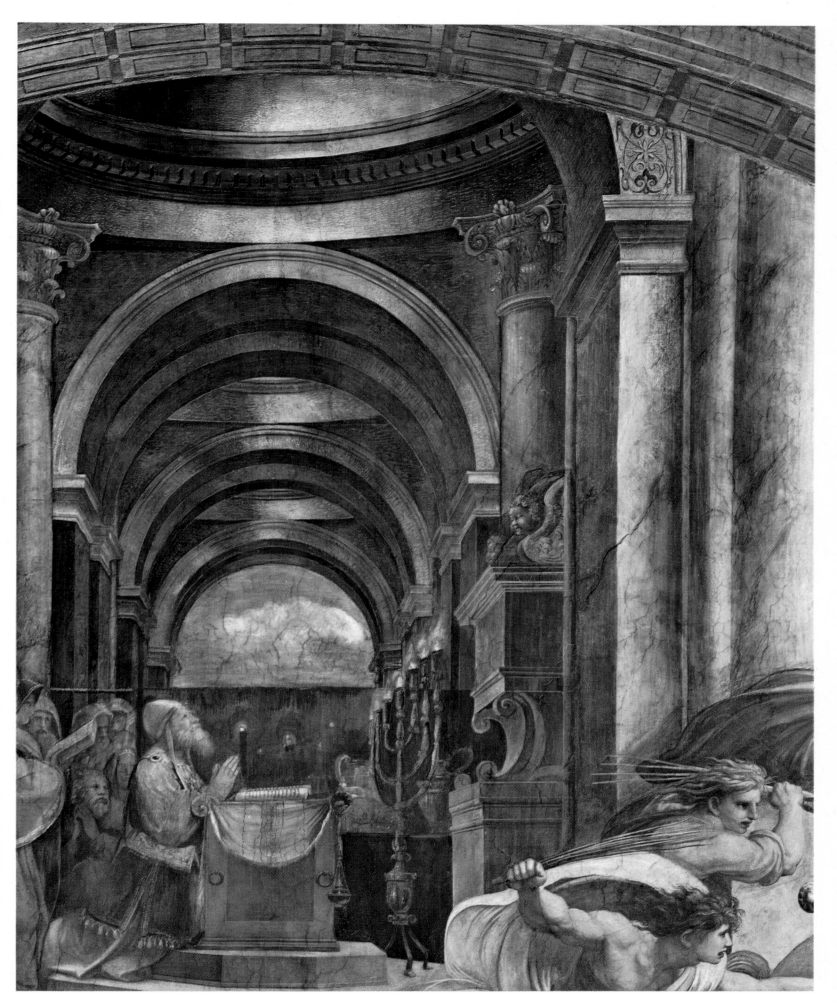

PLATE XXXIX   STANZA DI ELIODORO Vatican
Detail of *The Expulsion of Heliodorus from the Temple* (230 cm.)

PLATE XL   STANZA DI ELIODORO Vatican
Detail of *The Mass of Bolsena* (141 cm.)

PLATE XLI   STANZA DI ELIODORO Vatican
Detail of *The Mass of Bolsena* (188 cm.)

PLATE XLII STANZA DI ELIODORO Vatican
Detail of *The Mass of Bolsena* (94 cm.)

PLATE XLIII   STANZA DI ELIODORO Vatican
Detail of *The Mass of Bolsena* (136 cm.)

PLATE XLIV   STANZA DI ELIODORO Vatican
Detail of *The Mass of Bolsena* (71 cm.)

PLATE XLV STANZA DI ELIODORO Vatican
Detail of *The Liberation of St Peter* (235 cm.)

PLATE XLVI STANZA DI ELIODORO Vatican
Detail of *The Liberation of St Peter* (215 cm.)

PLATE XLVII STANZA DI ELIODORO Vatican
Detail of *The Liberation of St Peter* (220 cm.)

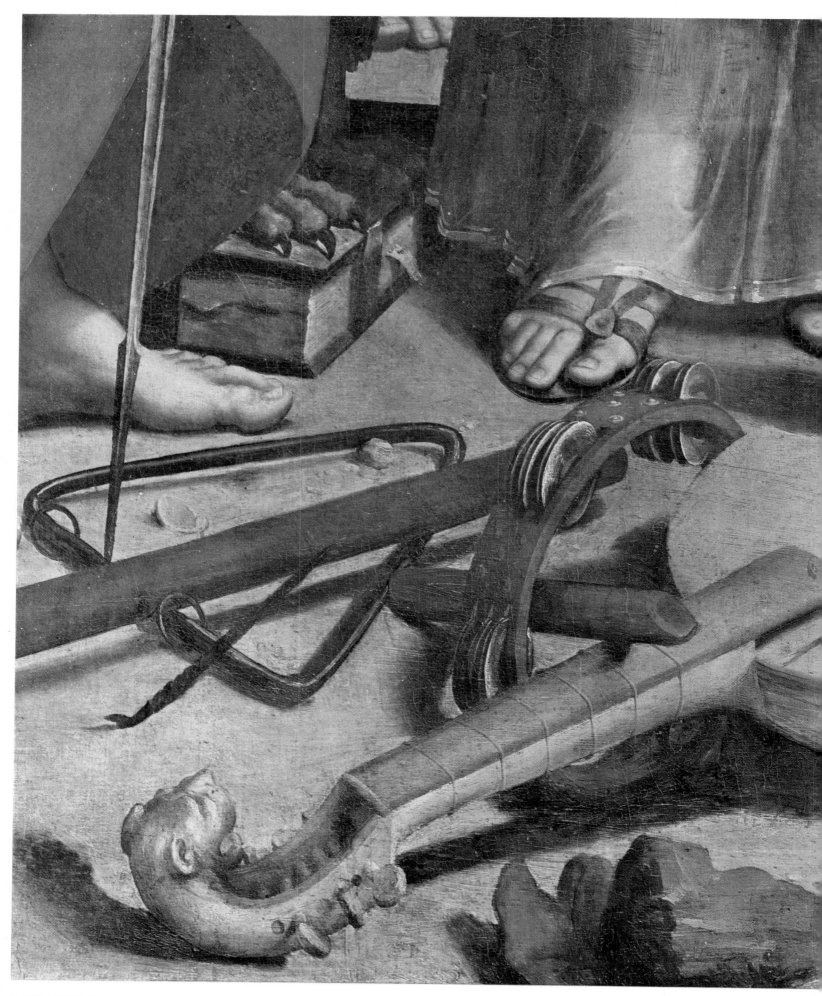

PLATES XLVIII-XLIX   THE ECSTASY OF ST CECILIA Bologna, Pinacoteca Nazionale
Detail (83 cm.)

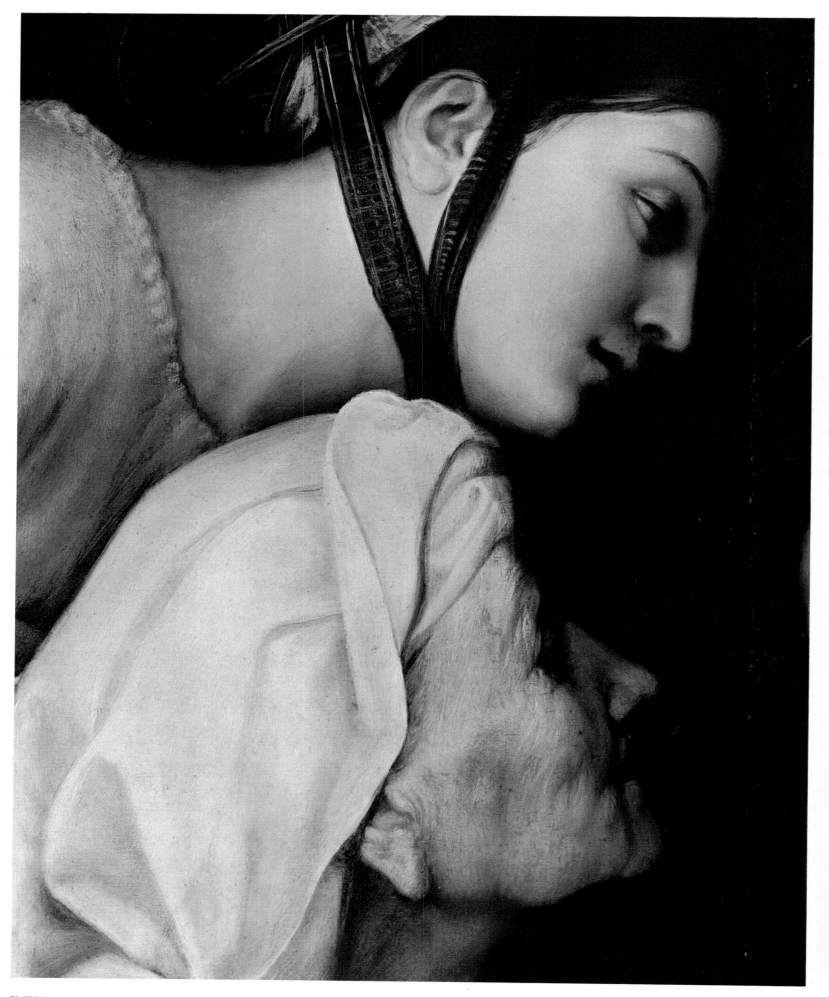

PLATE L   THE MADONNA OF THE LINEN WINDOW (DELL'IMPANNATA)   Florence, Pitti
Detail (30.4 cm.)

PLATE LI MADONNA AND SLEEPING CHILD WITH THE INFANT ST JOHN (MADONNA OF THE DIADEM) Paris, Louvre
Whole (44 cm.)

PLATE LII   MADONNA AND CHILD WITH THE INFANT ST JOHN (MADONNA OF THE CHAIR) Florence, Pitti
Whole (diam. 71 cm.)

PLATE LIII   PORTRAIT OF FEDRA INGHIRAMI   Florence, Pitti
Whole (62 cm.)

PLATE LIV   PORTRAIT OF BALDASSAR CASTIGLIONE   Paris, Louvre
Whole (67 cm.)

PLATE LV   PORTRAIT OF A WOMAN (THE LADY WITH A VEIL) Florence, Pitti
Whole (64 cm.)

PLATE LVI   THE SISTINE MADONNA Dresden, Gemäldegalerie
Whole (196 cm.)

PLATE LVII   THE VISION OF EZEKIEL Florence, Pitti
Whole (30 cm.)

PLATE LVIII   THE SPASIMO DI SICILIA Madrid, Prado
Detail (actual size)

PLATE LIX   THE LOGGIA DI PSICHE Rome, Farnesina
Whole (floor measurements: 19.3×7.5 metres)

PLATE LX   PORTRAIT OF LEO X WITH CARDINALS GIULIO DE' MEDICI AND LUIGI DE' ROSSI   Florence, Uffizi
Detail (35 cm.)

PLATE LXI   PORTRAIT OF LEO X WITH CARDINALS GIULIO DE' MEDICI AND LUIGI DE' ROSSI 'Florence, Uffizi
Detail (45 cm.)

PLATE LXII   PORTRAIT OF JOANNA OF ARAGON Paris, Louvre
Whole (95 cm.)

PLATE LXIII   PORTRAIT OF YOUNG WOMAN (THE FORNARINA) Rome, Galleria Nazionale
Whole (60 cm.)

PLATE LXIV   THE TRANSFIGURATION Rome, Pinacoteca Vaticana
Detail (147 cm.)

The Works

Key to symbols used

In order to provide, in readily accessible form, a guide to the basic elements of each work, all items of the Catalogue are preceded by a number (which refers to the chronological position of the work in the painter's activity, and is used throughout this publication for purposes of identification), and by a series of symbols denoting the following:
1 execution of the work, i.e. to what extent it is the artist's own work
2 medium
3 base
4 location
5 other information such as: whether the work is signed or dated; whether it is now complete; whether it was originally finished. The remaining numerals denote respectively the size, in centimetres, of the painting (height x width) and the date. These figures are preceded or followed by an asterisk in all cases in which the information given is approximate only. All such data are based on the general consensus of opinion in the field of modern art history. Outstanding differences of opinion and any further relevant data are discussed in the text.

1 *Execution*

⊞ Autograph

▦ Done by artist with assistance

▦ Done by artist and associates

▦ Done by artist with extensive help from associates

▦ Work executed in the bottega (workshop)

▦ Attributed to the artist by most authorities

▦ Attribution questioned by most authorities

▦ Traditionally attributed to artist

▦ Recently attributed to artist

2 *Medium*

◉ Oil

◉ Fresco

◉ Tempera

3 *Base*

◉ Panel

◉ Wall

◉ Canvas

4 *Location*

⦂ Premises open to the public

⦂ Private collection

⦂ Whereabouts unknown

⦂ Work lost

5 *Other data*

▤ Work signed

▤ Work dated

▤ Work incomplete or now fragmentary

▤ Work unfinished

⊞◉▤

6 Key to these symbols provided in the text

Bibliography

An important collection of sources and documents is found in V. Golzio's *Raffaello nei documenti, nelle testimonianze dei contemporanei e nella letteratura del suo secolo*, Vatican City 1936. The Raphael literature up to 1935 was noted by O. Fischel, *Santi Raffaello*, in KL (for list of abbreviations see below). Among the many works devoted to the artist should be mentioned: J. D. Passavant, *Raphael von Urbino und sein Vater Giovanni Santi*, Leipzig 1839–58; G. B. Cavalcaselle and J. A. Crowe, *Raffaello, la sua vita e le sue opere*, Florence 1884–91; E. Müntz, *Raphael, sa vie, son oeuvre et son temps*, Paris 1896; A. Rosenberg and G. Gronau, *Raphael*, Stuttgart-Leipzig 1909; O. Fischel, *Raffaels Zeichnungen*, Berlin 1913–41; S. Ortolani, *Raffaello*, Bergamo 1942; O. Fischel, *Raphael*, London 1948; E. Camesasca, *Tutta la pittura di Raffaello*, Milan 1956; W. Schöne, *Raphael*, Berlin-Darmstadt 1958. To these should be added the relevant passages in J. Lermolieff, *Die Werke Italienischer Meister in den Galerien von München, Dresden und Berlin*, Leipzig 1880 and B. Berenson, *The Central Italian Painters of the Renaissance*, London 1897 and *Italian Painters of the Renaissance*, Oxford 1932. Also H. Wölfflin, *Classic Art* (translated by P. and L. Murray), London 1952; F. Hartt, *Giulio Romano* (2 vols), Yale 1958 and S. J. Freedberg, *Painting of the High Renaissance in Rome and Florence* (2 vols), Harvard 1961. Among articles should be mentioned, for the formation and early period of Raphael's activity, that of R. Longhi, PA 1955; for the Stanze E. Wind, JWCI 1937–8 and 1938–9; D. Redig de Campos, IV 1938; *Raffaello e Michelangelo*, Rome 1946, *Le Stanze di Raffaello*, Florence 1950; A Chastel, *Art et Humanisme à Florence au temps de Laurent le Magnifique*, Paris 1959; C. G. Stridbeck, *Raphael Studies*, Stockholm 1960; K. Oberhuber, JKS 1962. For *The Sistine Madonna*: M. Putscher, *Raphaels Sixtinische Madonna*, Tübingen 1955 and M. Alpatov, A 1957. On *The Transfiguration*: K. Oberhuber, JBM 1962. On the Chigi Chapel: J. Shearman and M. Hirst, JWCI 1961, and for the Tapestry Cartoons: J. White and J. Shearman, AB 1958.

List of abbreviations

A : *L'Arte* (Rome, Turin, Milan)
AAM : *Arte antica e moderna* (Florence)
AB : *The Art Bulletin* (Washington, Providence)
AE : *Archaelogiai Értesitö* (Budapest)
AF : *Arte figurativa* (Milan)
AHAH : *Acta historiae artium Academiae Scientiarum Hungaricae* (Budapest)
AL : *Arte lombarda* (Milan)
AQ : *The Art Quarterly* (Detroit)
AS : *Les Arts* (Paris)
ASA : *Archivio storico dell'arte* (Rome)
ASRSP : *Archivio della Società Romana de Storia Patria* (Rome)
B : *Belfagor* (Messina, Florence)
BDA : *Bollettino d'arte* (Rome)
BDIA : *Bulletin of the Detroit Institute of Arts* (Detroit)
BICR : *Bollettino dell'Istituto centrale del restauro* (Rome)
BM : *The Burlington Magazine* (London)
C : *Commentari* (Florence)
CDA : *Critica d'arte* (Florence)
CEDA : *Cronache d'arte* (Bologna)
D : *Dedalo* (Milan)
EUA : *Enciclopedia universale dell'arte* (Venice, Rome)
FFR : *Festschrift für Max J Friedlaender* (Leipzig 1927)
GBA : *Gazette des Beaux-Arts* (Paris)
GEA : *Giornale de erudizione artistica* (Perugia)

GNI : *Le Gallerie nazionali italiane* (Rome)
IV : *Illustrazione vaticana* (Vatican City)
JBM : *Jahrbuch der Berliner Museum* (Berlin)
JKS : *Jahrbuch der Kunsthistorisches Sammlungen* (Vienna)
JPK : *Jahrbuch der Preussischen Kunstsammlungen* (Berlin)
JWCI : *Journal of the Warburg and Courtauld Institutes* (London)
K : *Kunstchronik* (Munich, Nuremberg)
KL : *Allgemeines Lexikon*, Thieme-Becker-Vollmer (Leipzig)
MFK : *Monatschefte für Kunstwissenschaft* (Leipzig)
MK : *Museumskunde* (Berlin, Leipzig)
NA : *Nuova Antologia* (Florence, Rome)
P : *Pinacotheca* (Rome)
PA : *Paragone* (Milan)
PT : *Pantheon* (Munich)
Q : *Quadrum* (Brussels)
RA : *Rassegna d'arte* (Milan)
RAAM : *Revue de l'arte ancien et moderne* (Paris)
RBAI : *Rassegna bibliografica dell'arte italiana* (Ascoli Piceno)
RDM : *Revue des Deux Mondes* (Paris)
RFK : *Repertorium für Kunstwissenschaft* (Berlin, Leipzig)
RPAA : *Atti della Pontificia Accademia Romana de Archeologia – Rendiconti*, (Vatican City)

SA : *SeleArte* (Florence)
SDW : *Studien der Bibliothek Warburg* (Hamburg)
VA : *Vita artistica* (Rome)
ZBK : *Zeitschrift für bildende Kunst* (Leipzig)

Outline Biography

1483 April 6 'At three o'clock in the night' (Vasari) in Urbino Raphael was born to Magia di Battista di Nicola Ciarla and her husband, the painter Giovanni di Sante di Pietro, a descendant of a Sante who lived in the early 14th century (hence, the patronymic 'Santi' or 'de' Santi' which Raphael later latinized to 'Santius' and 'Sanzio'. Vasari states that Raphael was born and died on Good Friday; in consequence, the date of birth has been taken as March 28 or 26, depending on whether one uses the astrological charts or the Julian calendar. However, the epitaph, attributed to Bembo, gives April 6 as the day of Raphael's death and birth. A letter from Michiel (see *1520*) confirms this date.

1491 October 7 Death of Raphael's mother; shortly after, Giovanni Santi marries a certain Bernadina and from this marriage is born a daughter Elizabeth. The paternal branch of the family are to have disputes with Raphael over financial matters concerning the two women.

1494 August 1 Giovanni Santi dies.

1500 A document relating to a disagreement with his step-mother reveals that Raphael was absent from Urbino on May 13. On December 10 Raphael and Pian di Meleto receive a commission for *The Coronation of St Nicholas of Tolentino* (see Catalogue, 13 A-D). The document setting out the commission not only places Raphael's name – 'Rafael Johannis Santis de Urbino' – before that of his older colleague, but gives him the title of 'magister'.

1501 September 13 'Magister Rafael Johannis Santis de Urbino et Vangelista Andree de Plano Meleti' have completed the above mentioned altarpiece.

1501–3 During this period, the Abbess of the Convent of Monteluce in Perugia commissions Raphael to paint the *Coronation* (156).

1503 The date MDIII is found on an inscription relating to the Mond Crucifixion (23 A)

1504 The date MDIIII appears on *The Marriage of the Virgin* in Milan (Catalogue, 28). On October 1 Giovanna Feltria, wife of Giovanni della Rovere, sends a letter of recommendation to Gonfalonier Soderini of Florence: 'Raphael, a painter from Urbino of considerable talent, would like to move to Florence.'

1505 The fresco in the Church of S. Severo in Perugia (Catalogue, 80) bears the date MDV, which some critics judge as either false or a late addition. The same date was read on the *Madonna del Prato* (63). On December 12 the panel for the Monteluce *Coronation* had not yet been prepared. On the 23rd of that same month Raphael receives thirty ducats on account for this altarpiece.

1506 The date MDVI appears on the Ansidei Altarpiece (Catalogue, 46 A and B).

1507 The date MDVII appears on the Baglioni Altarpiece (Catalogue, 70 A-C). The same date has been detected on *The Holy Family with the Lamb* and *La Belle Jardinière* (71 and 69). In May *The Agony in the Garden* (now lost) was probably finished (59). On October 11 Raphael's presence in Urbino is recorded in a legal document. In the *Diarium* of the papal Master of Ceremonies, Paris de Grassis, we learn that on the day of his coronation, Julius II expressed his unwillingness to inhabit the Borgia apartments to avoid seeing the portrait of his predecessor, Alexander VI.

1508 The date MDVII is written on the large Cowper Madonna (Catalogue, 82). On April 21 Raphael writes to his uncle Simone Ciarla in Florence. Malvasia (1678) published another letter, which Raphael is supposed to have sent to Francesco Francia from Rome on September 5.

Raphael's signature on The Marriage of the Virgin *(28) in Milan.*

Raphael's transfer from Tuscany to Rome is therefore presumed to have occurred at some time between the dates of the two letters. Contemporary critics, however, generally regard the second letter as false.

1509 A document dated January 13 provides the first definite proof of Raphael's presence in Rome. On October 4 he receives the honorary nomination of writer of 'briefs'.

1510 November 10 Two bronze tondos with flowers in bas-relief were executed by the goldsmith Cesare Rossetti after drawings of Raphael.

1511 The date MDXI is inscribed on *Parnassus* and *The Virtues* in the Stanza della Segnatura (Catalogue, 85 K and N). A letter sent to Isabella d'Este on August 16 from G.F. Grossi states that Julius II wants a portrait of Federico Gonzaga, hostage of the papal court, 'in a room which the Pope is having painted in the Vatican.'

1512 The date MDXII can be read under *The Mass of Bolsena* (Catalogue, 95 F). On May 24 Isabella d'Este wrote to Matteo Ippolito to request 'Raphaello de Zoanne de Sancto' to paint a portrait of Federico Gonzaga 'dal pecto in suso armato.'

1513 January 11 – February 19 Letters to the court of Mantua from envoys to the Curia relate that Raphael was engaged on a portrait of Federico Gonzaga (Catalogue, 102). On July 7, he receives fifty ducats from the treasury of Leo X (elected on March 11) presumably for the Stanza decorations.

1514 Elena, wife of Benedetto dall'Oglio, commissioned Raphael to paint the Bologna *St Cecilia* (Catalogue, 108). On April 1 Raphael is provisionally nominated architect of St Peter's at 300 ducats a year as Bramante's assistant. On July 1 he writes to his uncle Ciarla. He receives a final payment on August 1 of one hundred ducats 'for the painting of the new rooms' (the Stanza). On that same date, a brief from Leo X confirms his appointment as architect of St Peter's, as the successor to Bramante. The date August 15 appears in a letter from Raphael to Marco Fabio Calvo (which some critics consider false). This period also includes the letter to Baldassare Castiglione with the well-known passage about 'the famine of beautiful women' which Raphael overcomes in his painting by resorting to 'a certain idea that springs from my mind.'

1515 A drawing by Raphael in the Albertina in Vienna, related to *The Battle of Ostia* (Catalogue, 115 B), is dated 1515 in a note in Dürer's handwriting, which states that the drawing was sent by Raphael to his colleague in Nuremberg. In two letters to Isabella d'Este, one dated June 7 from Agostino Gonzaga and another on November 8 from Castiglione, and in a third letter (November 30) in reply to Castiglione, reference is made to a small painting which the Duchess wished to have from Raphael. An order of payment of June 15 provides the first information on the Vatican tapestries (116 A-J). Raphael is nominated keeper of Roman antiquities by the Pope on August 27. A document dated November 8, regarding his purchase of a house in the Borgo, reveals that Raphael was absent from Rome. It can be assumed that he was summoned to Florence, together with the principle architects of Italy, in connection with the project for

Supposed self-portrait as a youth (Oxford, Ashmolean Museum). Subsequent self-portraits — other than that in the Uffizi (54) in 39, 85J, 91, 95E (the bearer of the pope's chair at left), 120 and 143.

the façade of S. Lorenzo. His presence in Florence is mentioned by Bandinelli in a letter to Cosimo I on December 7.

1516 This date appears on the mosaics of the Chigi Chapel in Sta Maria del Popolo in Rome, executed by De Pace from drawings by Raphael. At approximately this date, Cardinal Gregorio Cortesi writes to Raphael: 'Raphaelem pictorem aetate nostra, ut nostri, veteribus illis excellentissimis comparandum', requesting, in vain, that he fresco the refectory of the convent of S.Polidoro in Modena. In a letter of April 3 Bembo announces to Bibbiena 'Tomorrow I shall go to Tivoli again . . . with Navagiero and Beazzano and M. Baldassar Castiglione and Raphael. We shall see the old and the new and all that is beautiful in that region.' In a letter of April 19, Bembo reports to Bibbiena: 'Raphael has done a portrait of our Tebaldeo which is so true to life that it resembles the original as much as the original does.' Further, Raphael requests the cardinal 'to send him a list of the other subjects which are to be depicted in your stufetta' (Catalogue, 125). The same letter also mentions the portrait of Castiglione (114) and 'our Duke', which has been

variously identified (57). In a letter dated May 6, Bembo reports to Bibbiena, 'the stufetta is being prepared and it will indeed be very beautiful . . . the new rooms (Stanze 85 A-P, 95 A-H, 115 A-D) have been prepared and the loggia as well' (Vatican, second floor 149 A-M). A document dated May 23 shows that Valerio Porcari owes Raphael over a thousand florins, for reasons unknown. On June 8 Raphael's name was inscribed in the epigraph on the tomb of the elephant Annone (126). On June 20 Bembo announces to Bibbiena the completion of the Stufetta. The next day the contract for the Monteluce *Coronation* (156) is renewed. On July 7 Benedetto Calilupi writes to Isabella d'Este about some silver basins designed by Raphael. In a letter to Michelangelo on November 22, Leonardo Sellaio refers to a putto modelled in clay by Raphael and copied in marble by Pietro d'Ancona. On December 20 Raphael receives the final payment for the Vatican tapestry cartoons.

1517 Castiglione composes two sonnets for the portrait of a 'most beautiful and noble' lady (Salvadori in *Il Cortegiano*, 1884) by Raphael. It appears from a document dated January 10 that Raphael contracted a loan of 150 ducats from the banker Bernardo Bini. In a letter to Michelangelo on January 19, Leonardo Sellaio refers to Raphael's commission for *The Transfiguration* (Catalogue, 153), which coincided, to Raphael's dismay, with one to Sebastiano del Piombo for a *Raising of Lazarus.* 'I think Raphael will raise Heaven and earth to try and stop him (Piombo) from carrying out his commission, as he is afraid of competing with him.' A long and extensive correspondence between the envoy Bertrando Costabile and the Duke of Ferrara begins on March 21, concerning *The Triumph of Bacchus* which Raphael was supposed to paint for the duke. We learn from one of the letters (June 16) that Raphael's *Incendio* (115 A-D) is near completion. On July 10 Raphael's apprentices receive twenty ducats for having painted the room preceding the wardrobe (possibly the Hall of the Grooms, 131). In a letter to Cardinal Bibbiena, Bembo declares 'the rooms (Stanze) that Raphael decorated for His Holiness are very beautiful thanks to the singular and excellent paintings.' On September 24 Porcari settles his debt to Raphael for one hundred ducats. According to a deed dated October 7 (Rome, Archivio Capitolino) Raphael purchased for 3,000 ducats Palazzo Caprini in the Borgo, which Vasari asserts was constructed by Bramante for Raphael. In November Raphael sends the cartoon for one of the frescoes in the Sala dell'Incendio (115 B) to the Duke of Ferrara, hoping to stay in his good graces despite the delay in the execution of *The Triumph of Bacchus*. On the 6th of the same month Lorenzo de' Medici, Duke of Urbino, requests Raphael to design a coin.

1518 On January 1 Leonardo Sallaio announced to Michelangelo the completion of the Farnesina loggia (Catalogue, 130), 'a despicable thing for a great master, far worse than the last Stanza'. Several letters dated between January 22 and February 5 refer to the completion of the portrait of Lorenzo de' Medici (p. 124). A payment of thirty-two ducats was made to Raphael in March 'per l'opera della Loggia' (Vatican, second floor, 149 A–M). According to Lacroix (cited by Passavant) the word 'Loggia' is actually 'Robbia', and refers to some glazed terracotta for a floor, possibly in the Logge. Between March and June 19 several letters from various people mention the *St Michael* and the *Holy Family* for François I (135 & 136), which were completed on May 27. On April 20 payment is made 'for carriage of eleven tapestries from Lyon to here' (Rome), for the Sistine Chapel (116). On May 15 Raphael buys a vineyard in Rome. (see *1519*). In a letter to Michelangelo on July 2, Sebastiano del Piombo reports that Raphael has not yet begun *The Transfiguration*, and refers to the two works for François I as 'painted by the prince of the Synagogue' (alluding to Raphael's avarice). He continues: 'You can not imagine anything more contrary to your ideas . . . the figures look smoky, or as though made of metal, all darks and lights.' In another letter to Michelangelo on July 20, Domenico Menighella relates that Raphael wished to send *The Transfiguration* to France to complete the gilding. Sebastiano del Piombo objected, hoping to finish *The Raising of Lazarus* by mid-August and win the competition. In a letter to the Duke of Ferrara on August 13, the envoy Costabile mentions Raphael's heavy commitments as an architect and painter and says that the duke must therefore realize the difficulties in completing *The Triumph of Bacchus*, for which Raphael had recently received fifty ducats on account. Between September 21 and November 20 numerous letters on this subject were exchanged. One letter dated September 22 relates that one of Raphael's apprentices (presumably Battista Dossi) is going to Venice . . . 'I believe to buy paints.' On November 10 the *St Michael* cartoon (135) reaches Ferrara in an attempt by Raphael to pacify the duke. The letters recommence on December 29 (continuing until March 2) and Raphael tries to stave off the duke's entreaties by sending the cartoon for *Joanna of Aragon* (142). Possibly that same year, or shortly after, Raphael and Antonio da Sangallo the Younger, appointed 'Masters of the Street', were studying city planning in Rome.

1519 Raphael sends Leo X the famous memorandum, drawn up by Castiglione, on the preservation of classical monuments in Rome, and the map of ancient Rome. Between February 17 and March 8 and between April 30 and September 21, numerous letters refer to *The Triumph of Bacchus*. In one letter dated late February, Gerolamo da Bagnacavallo claims to have seen the sketches, which he describes as very beautiful. Another letter dated March 8 refers to the stage set prepared by Raphael for Ariosto's *Gli Suppositi* : 'it is very beautiful and represents 'Ferrara in perspective'.' on May 4 Marcantonio Michiel writes to Antonio Marsilio in Venice : 'Raphael of Urbino has painted a very long loggia in the Vatican' (on the seond floor) (Catalogue, 149 A–M), and went straight on to paint two others which will be of exceptional beauty (150 and 151). On May 7 Raphael received 400 ducats from the papal treasury and was credited with an additional 600. On June 3 Castiglione writes to Federico Gonzaga that Raphael has executed the drawings of *The Entombment* (no further identification given), presumably requested by Gonzaga. On June 11 the papal treasury pays twenty-five ducats to Raphael's apprentices 'who painted the loggia' (149 A–M). Castiglione records the completion of this undertaking : 'it could not be more beautiful', in a letter to Isabella d'Este on June 16. Sanuto makes an entry in his *Diarii* in July about the proposal by Raphael, 'a worthy and intelligent painter and architect', to transport an obelisk, discovered near the Tomb of Augustus, to St Peter's Square for 90,000 ducats. We also learn from Sanuto that three of the Sistine Chapel tapestries had already been brought to Rome. In a document of August 28 Agostino Chigi engages Raphael to build a family chapel in the Church of Sta Maria del Popolo. This same document indicates that the Chigi Chapel in Sta Maria della Pace is still unfinished. (It must have been near completion, however, since a memorial stone records the year of dedication as MDXIX.) In Paris de Grassis' *Diarium* on December 26, he refers to the tapestries displayed in the

Portrait of Raphael (engraving) by M. A. Raimondi.

Sistine Chapel. In a note dated the following day, Michiel specifies that there were seven tapestries and an eighth was being prepared. We also learn that 'during the past few days the lower loggia in the Vatican was prepared' (150).

1520 Between January 20 and March 21, there is another series of letters concerning *The Triumph of Bacchus*. One dated March 20 states that Raphael is engaged in designing some fireplaces (or mantelpieces) for Alfonso I d'Este. On January 29 Pandolfo Pico della Mirandola writes from Rome to the Duchess of Mantua that he has met a Florentine painter about twenty years old, who grew up in the school of Michelangelo, but since Raphael keeps him in an inferior position, Pico della Mirandola has suggested that he leave Rome. Morelli (*Die Galerien Borghese . . .*, 1890) imagines that the artist in question is Perino del Vaga.

Raphael dies on April 6. The same day Michiel reports the general bereavement, including the pope's, and notes that the dead man's estate was assessed at 16,000 ducats. He adds that Raphael was especially mourned by the men of letters, because of the unfinished state of his description and painting of ancient Rome (see *1519*). News of Raphael's death is also sent by Michiel to Antonio Marsilio with the remark that Raphael's death plunged the entire papal court into grief and was accompanied by signs like those which occurred at the death of Christ ; a crack appeared in the Vatican Palace, and the building came near to collapse. Pandolfo Pico della Mirandola's letter to the Duchess of Mantua is written in the same tone, as is Germanello's letter to Federico Gonzaga. On April 12 Sebastiano del Piombo writes to Michelangelo : 'I believe you know how that poor fellow Raphael of Urbino died and I believe you were much grieved. May God have mercy on him.' Several days before, on April 7, Alfonso d'Este was informed by his agent Paolucci : 'Today Raphael of Urbino was buried in the Pantheon, having died of a violent and unabated fever.' This seems a more likely cause of death than the excesses of an erotic nature mentioned by Vasari.

At some time in April Paolucci receives instructions from the Duke of Ferrara to obtain a refund of the amount paid in advance to Raphael for *The Triumph of Bacchus*. An extensive exchange of letters ensues. On April 16 Isabella d'Este replies to Pico della Mirandola (see above) : 'I am much grieved to hear of Raphael's death.' Sebastiano del Piombo writes to Michelangelo on July 3 that Raphael's apprentices were commissioned to continue the decoration of the Sala di Costantino in the Vatican where they had painted on the walls, as a sample, a very fine figure in oil (Catalogue, 154 E). In Bibbiena's will of November

8, there is a reference to a painting of the Virgin by Raphael, intended for Castiglione. On December 29 Castiglione writes to his mother in Mantua to announce the sending of a 'painting of Our Lady by the hand of Raphael.'

1521 The Duke of Ferrara receives the amount advanced to Raphael for *The Triumph of Bacchus*. A letter from Castiglione to Federico Gonzaga on December 16 relates that the Sala di Costantino is more than half decorated (154 A–F).

1522 On May 7 Castiglione writes to Cardinal Giulio de' Medici, who commissioned *The Transfiguration* (Catalogue, 153), to settle the account with Giulio Romano who has completed it.

Supposed self-portrait by Raphael (engraving) by W. Hollar.

1523 *The Transfiguration* is placed in the church of S. Pietro in Montorio, as recorded by an inscription, published by Bottari. Two letters from Castiglione in Mantua request his administrator in Rome, A. Piperario, to apply to Giulio Romano for a certain painting by Raphael belonging to Master Antonio di S. Marino, and on May 8 to inquire whether Romano still has 'that puttino in marble by Raphael', and how much he wants for it.

1524 Summonte replies to Michiel, concerning Raphael's works in Naples, with information about *The Madonna of the Fish* (Catalogue, 111) in the church of S.Domenico, 'in the chapel of Signor Ioan Baptista del Duce.' On September 5 Castiglione announces to the Duke of Mantua that the Sala di Costantino is very beautiful. Between November 13 and August 11, 1525, various letters passed concerning the portrait of Leo X (145), desired by Federico II Gonzaga and promised to him – through Aretino's intercession – by Clement VII, subject to the execution of a copy in Florence. The progress of the negotiations is documented up to the making of preparations for the sending of the painting to Mantua ; however, it is not known whether Gonzaga ever received it (see *1531*). Moreover, Vasari maintains that a copy, not the original, was sent.

1525 See *1524*.

1525 January 18–April 5. Baldassare da Pescia receives 200 ducats as final payment for *The Transfiguration* (Catalogue, 153).

1527 *Antiquitates Urbis* of Andrea Fulvio is published. The dedication to the pope contains a reference to the map of ancient Rome begun by Raphael a few days before his death.

1531 October 28 In a letter to Federico Gonzaga, the administrator Ippolito Calandra mentions that among Gonzaga's possessions, besides a painting of Leo X (no further information is given and it can therefore only be conjectured whether this work is identifiable with the portrait executed by Raphael) is a painting that 'Raphael of Urbino did for Your Excellency.' This work has been identified with the *La Perla* (Catalogue, 155).

1538 July 29 In a letter to M. A. Anselmi, Bembo states that he is going to give Beazzano the 'double portrait by Raphael' (Catalogue, 123), mentioned by Michiel c. 1525 in Padua in the house of Bembo.

1570 August 26 – September 9 Letters are exchanged between the monks of the Camaldolese monastery and Guidobaldo II of Urbino regarding their offer for *The Agony in the Garden* (Catalogue, 59) owned by Guidobaldo.

1571 August 10 Antonio Dosio writes to an unidentified person about a cartoon by Raphael.

1583 January 22 Cardinal Delfino in Rome sends an *Annunciation* by Raphael to Bianca, Grand Duchess of Tuscany (see p. 124).

Catalogue of works

Raphael received his introduction to painting from his father, Giovanni Santi, who died in 1494 'not a very exceptional painter, but a man of intellect' (Vasari). The most fundamental influence on Raphael's formation came from the artistic and literary society of Urbino, which was still under the domination of Laurana, Piero della Francesca and Francesco di Giorgio Martini. Raphael's apprenticeship to Perugino at the turn of the 15th century served as a means of recapturing a final echo of the art of Piero della Francesca, of discovering the secret of rigorous spatial articulation, and a sense of monumental composition.

Perugino's style is clearly reflected in Raphael's work prior to 1504 and, as Longhi points out, the years 1501–2 show the undeniable if faint influence of the brilliant and ornate principles of Pinturicchio. Even in his earliest works, Raphael displays some originality in his compositions, especially in the classic simplicity with which the architectural form and the feeling for space are emphasized. The best expression of this style is *The Marriage of the Virgin* in the Brera.

Raphael settled in Florence in the autumn of 1504. However, it is evident that, from his many

1

commissions from Umbria and Urbino, Raphael did not break off contact with Perugia and his native Urbino. For four years he devoted himself almost exclusively to an intense and detailed study of the Florentine tradition in an attempt to bring his style up to date with the most recent works of Leonardo and Michelangelo, as well as going back to the sources of inspiration of the 15th century: Pollaiuolo, Donatello and Della Robbia. Almost all of Raphael's output during these years – the large number of elaborate variations on the themes of the Madonna and

Child and the Holy Family and the portraits – bears the imprint of his study of Leonardo, and are the result of a profound meditation on Leonardo's search for complex solutions to problems of composition. These early works reveal Raphael's ability to fuse a convincing space with a new freedom of rhythm in his handling of groups of figures. Raphael further emphasizes the sheer beauty of colour and of landscape. The Florentine revival spent itself in a few years. With the departure of Michelangelo for Rome, and Leonardo for Milan, the intellectual brilliance of the early years of the century began to wane.

Towards the end of 1508 Raphael moved to Rome where Bramante introduced him to the papal court. The Rome of Julius II aspired to a universal renewal under the aegis of the Church and a rapid achievement of *plenitudo temporum* ('the fulness of time'). Florence could no longer offer Raphael an environment of such historical and human richness. Rome had inherited from Florence the position of cultural and artistic centre of the Renaissance.

Raphael managed to gain immediate access to the heart of the cultural activity in Rome and expressed the still unformulated ideals and aspirations of the humanists at the papal court and of the pope himself. The tone of serene intellectual meditation and the doctrine mirrored in the frescoes of the Stanza della Segnatura were followed in the second Stanza by a more expressly political theme. Raphael's frescoes become more excited, dramatic and more historical. They are rich in contrasting movements, with strong and powerful effects of light. But the political and religious motivations and ambitions of Julius II's era faded during the papacy of Leo X. The new pope was less a man of action than his predecessor, and surrounded himself with an extremely learned and splendid court in a culture of an erudite and classical character. By re-evoking the splendours of ancient Rome, Leo X was building the prestige of the new papal Rome.

Once again Raphael knew how to take command of the new situation. He left to his assistants the execution of most of the third Stanza's frescoes, which are conceived in an overtly commemorative tone, and continued in his altarpieces to achieve the revolutionary effects seen in *The Sistine Madonna, St Cecilia* and *The*

Transfiguration. In the tapestry (Arazzi) cartoons he retells the dramatic story of the second Stanza in a more forceful and eloquent form.

During the last years of his life, Raphael concentrated on architecture and the creation of a new type of fresco and stucco decoration, inspired by classical examples and intimately related to architectural form. His studies of Roman antiquities led him to conceive the scheme which was celebrated by the humanists and poets, of drawing up a plan of ancient Rome. By about 1514, Raphael's collaborators had begun to play an important role in the execution of his many commissions. This situation arose because of the pressure of the work which he undertook. Raphael, however, retained control of the planning of all

3

these commissions. Raphael's ever-growing activity as an architect contributed substantially to altering his relationship with his collaborators.

1   87 × 82   1495
Dead Christ Galleria Nazionale dell'Umbria, Perugia
The lunette from the Decemviri altarpiece (Pinacoteca Vaticana) painted by Perugino around 1495; formerly in the chapel of S. Ercolano in Perugia. Attributed to Raphael by A. Venturi (*Storia . . .*, 1913, VII 2) and by Galassi (NA, 1913); today unanimously regarded as by Perugino.

2   435 × 794   1495
The Last Supper From the Convent of S. Onofrio, Florence
When discovered under a layer of plaster in 1845, it was attributed to Raphael, a theory supported by numerous nineteenth-century critics: Foster, Masi, Montazio, Reaumont, Vitet, Milanesi, Bartalesi. Contemporary opinion is almost entirely agreed that it is by Perugino.

3   59 × 46   1495-96
Portrait of Perugino Uffizi, Florence
Catalogued by the Uffizi in 1704 as a portrait of Martin Luther by Holbein. Audin identified it in 1825 in his edition of Vasari's *Lives*, as the portrait of Verrocchio by Lorenzo di Credi, mentioned by Vasari. In 1922 A. Venturi (A),

2

followed by Gnoli and Canuti, attributed this work to Perugino, but still considered it a portrait of Verrocchio. Degenhart (PT), revived the attribution to Credi in 1931 ; Offner (BM, 1934), Beenken (ZBK, 1935) and Ortolani, on the other hand, claimed this was a portrait of Perugino painted by Raphael about 1506. Camesasca has rightly supported the Perugino attribution, and pointed out the connection between this work and the portrait of Francesco delle Opere, c. 1495–6. The portrait's strong resemblance to Perugino's self-portrait at the Cambio leaves little doubt as to the identity of the sitter.

4 ⊞ ⊕ 25×50 / 1497 ▤ ⁝
The Nativity Church of Sta Maria Nuova, Fano
One of the five panels from the predella of the altarpiece painted by Perugino ; commissioned for Sta Maria Nuova in Fano and completed in 1497. Formerly, the whole predella was attributed to Raphael, a theory supported by Durand Gréville (RAAM, 1907) ; Cavalcaselle considers the predella the main inspiration for Raphael's Vatican Coronation (24A). Later, the whole predella was regarded as a work of Perugino assisted by other painters. A.Venturi attributed it to Andrea di Assisi. More recently, in 1955, Longhi pointed out the

4

resemblance between the figure of the woman holding the newborn girl in The Nativity and The Madonna and Child in the Casa Santi in Urbino (6) ; he concludes that this particular panel represents a collaboration between the young Raphael and Perugino.

The Cambio Frescoes

5 ⊞ ⊕ *110×75* / 1498 ▤ ⁝
A. Fortitude
The first allusion to Raphael's part in the decoration of the hall of the Collegio del Cambio in Perugia goes back to a seventeenth-century manuscript (Lancellotti, *Scorta sacra*, Perugia, Biblioteca Civica), which refers to a young man from Urbino intent on 'decorating the ceiling with arabesques and rapidly painting the head of Christ Transfigured in the wondrous fashion of a true master.' Crispolti (*Perugia augusta*, 1648), considered the

The Cambio God the Father with Angels and Prophets. *All of the heavenly group, the figure of Solomon to the left and the group of prophets to the right (5 B - D), have been attributed to Raphael.*

possibility of Raphael's contribution, and Siepi and Gambini brought up the question again in the 19th century. In 1913 A.Venturi identified Raphael's contribution in the figure of Fortitude on the left wall and in the panel on the opposite wall, depicting God the Father flanked by two angels and various cherubs with a group of sibyls below. Gnoli (RA, 1913) accepts only the first part of this proposition ; Tacchi (*Rinascimento in Umbria*, 1945), Pittaluga and Fischel are in agreement with Venturi, and Fischel also includes the head of Solomon as Raphael's. Although other critics have rejected the possibility of attributing specific parts of the Cambio's decoration to Raphael ; they accept the possibility of his collaboration as an assistant.

Cavalcaselle regards this as a work of Giovanni Santi, portraying his son asleep in his mother's lap. Many favoured this opinion, including A.Venturi ; but recently many critics have returned to the original attribution. Longhi notes the likeness of the Madonna's profile to that of one of the attendant women in *The Nativity* from Perugino's altarpiece in Fano (4).

The Charity Standard

7 ⊞ ⊕ 112×66 / 1499 ▤ ⁝
A. The Crucifixion
The Crucifixion and the *Madonna della Misericordia* (7 B) make up the two sides of a standard painted for the Brotherhood of Charity in Città del Castello. It passed to the Pinacoteca Comunale from the Hospital of Mercy. First attributed by Mancini (*Istruzione . . . per . . . Città di Castello*, 1832), to the school of Perugino, then by Guardabassi (*Indiceguida . . . dell'Umbria*, 1872) to Francesco di Castello.

Camesasca noted that the areas attributed to Raphael are of superior quality, and are probably those where Perugino worked, having begun with Fortitude (1498) and completed the cycle in 1500 with the opposite wall.

5 ⊞ ⊕ 229×370 / 1500 ▤ ⁝
B. Father Between Angels and Cherubs
See 5 A.

5 ⊞ ⊕ 1500 ▤ ⁝
C. Sibyl
See 5 A.

5 ⊞ ⊕ 1500 ▤ ⁝
D. Solomon
See 5 A.

6 ⊞ ⊕ 97×67 / 1498-99 ▤ ⁝
Madonna and Child Casa Santi, Urbino
Though traditionally considered a very early work of Raphael,

In 1922 Longhi assigned the standard to Raphael. This attribution, which was published in 1922 in *Piero della Francesca*, reappeared in the catalogue *Casa italiana nei secoli* ('The Italian House Through the Centuries'), Florence, 1948, and was subsequently reaffirmed by Longhi himself (PA, 1955), who drew attention to the presence of Peruginesque elements and of elements deriving from the Urbino school, followers of Piero della Francesca, and dated the work approximately at the end of the 15th century.

7 ⊞ ⊕ 112×66 / 1499 ▤ ⁝
B. Madonna della Misericordia
See 7 A

8 ⊞ ⊕ 1499 ▤ ▢ ⁝
The Resurrection Private Collection, London
The picture was first published by Suida (AQ, 1955), who claimed that it belonged to the school of Perugino and was derived from Perugino's

altarpiece, commissioned in March 1499 for the Church of S. Francesco in Perugia and now in the Vatican Museums. Bologna (*Studies . . . dedicated to W. Suida*, 1959) then argued that the painting was by Raphael, and dated it to the same year as the Vatican *Resurrection*, 1499, but this is not widely accepted.

9 ⊞ ⊕ 53×41 / 1500* ▤ ⁝
Madonna of the Book Galleria Nazionale dell'Umbria, Perugia
Originally painted for the Church of Sta Maria della Misericordia in Perugia, it was attributed by A.Venturi to Eusebio da San Giorgio.

6

8

7A

7B

9

11

12

Detail of the head of St Nicholas from the preparatory drawing for The Coronation of St Nicholas of Tolentino (13) (Musée Wicar, Lille).

A partial eighteenth-century copy of The Coronation of St Nicholas (13) (Pinacoteca Civica, Città di Castello).

Berenson, followed by Volpe in 1962, described this as an early work of Raphael. Santi's (*La Galleria Nazionale . . . in Perugia*, 1955) and Camesasca's opinion that this is not by Raphael, but by a poor imitator, is convincing.

10 ⊞ ⊕ 1500* 🗐 ⦂
Predella, Subject Unknown
In an anonymous manuscript belonging to the Church of S. Francesco di Siena (Milanesi, in Vasari III), *The Nativity*, painted by Pinturicchio about 1500 for this church, is described as accompanied by a predella by Raphael.

11 ⊞ ⊕ 1500 - 01 🗐 ⦂
The Virgin Appears to a Man in Prayer Wainstein Collection, Helsinki
Once part of the William Dyce, D. Nathan and R. Langton Douglas collections in England, this work was shown at the Royal Academy of London. A. Venturi identified it as a panel from a predella by Raphael (A, 1928), executed around 1500–1. He reaffirmed his theory in *Raphael* (revised by L. Venturi in 1952), but the attribution has not been accepted by other scholars.

12 ⊞ ⊕ 224×162 1501 🗐 ⦂
The Resurrection Pinacoteca Vaticana, Rome
Commissioned from Perugino in 1499 for the Church of S. Francesco al Prato in Perugia and probably completed in 1506. It was requisitioned by the French in 1797 and transferred to Paris ; it was returned to the Vatican in 1815. Cavalcaselle's theory that Raphael collaborated extensively with Perugino was strengthened by relating this work to two drawings attributed to Raphael (Ashmolean Museum, Oxford). These were later correctly identified with the São Paulo *Resurrection* (18) by Regteren van Altena in 1927. Any contribution by Raphael has been excluded.

The Coronation of St Nicholas of Tolentino

Commissioned on December 10, 1500 for the Baronci Chapel in the Church of S. Agostino in Città di Castello from Raphael and Evangelista da Pian di Meleto, and completed on September 13, 1501. Seriously damaged by an earthquake in 1789, the fragments were purchased that same year by Pius VI and remained in the Vatican until 1849 when they were dispersed. It is possible to reconstruct the altarpiece from a free adaptation, formerly in the Augustinian Convent in Città del Castello and now in the Pinacoteca, probably dating from the 18th century, and from the preparatory drawings in the Musée Wicar in Lille.

Behind the central figures, a large archway opens onto the countryside in the foreground, flanked by two angels on the right and one on the left, all bearing screeds ; St Nicholas stands with a foot on the fallen Satan. In the upper register, God the Father, holding a crown, is placed between the Madonna and St Augustine, both of whom hold crowns. The general conception of the altarpiece was Raphael's, as is revealed by the Lille drawings. Their superior quality and greater fluency, compared with Perugino's style, was noted by Fischel, Longhi and Brizio. The following paintings represent the remaining fragments of the altarpiece.

13 ⊞ ⊕ 31×27 1500 - 01 🗐 ⦂
A. An Angel Pinacoteca Tosio Martinengo, Brescia
Originally attributed to Timoteo Viti, Fischel (JPK, 1912) recognized it after it had been cleaned by Cavenaghi as a Raphael and as part of the St Nicholas altarpiece (one of the

13A

13B

13C

13D

14

angels to the right). This attribution is generally accepted.

13 ⊞ ⊕ 112×115 1500 - 01 🗐 ⦂
B. God the Father and Cherubs The Madonna Galleria Nazionale di Capodimonte, Naples
These two fragments, which have now been rejoined, were identified in 1912 by Fischel, together with the Tosio *Angel* (13A) as works of Raphael. Fischel's theory was well received by the critics, including Pittaluga, who considered these two fragments of a superior quality to the Tosio Angel.

13 ⊞ ⊕ 1500 - 01 🗐 ⦂
C. St Nicholas Resuscitates Two Doves Institute of Arts, Detroit
This set of two panels (13 D) in the Detroit Institute was identified by Berenson in 1896 as miraculous scenes from the life of St Francis by Eusebio di San Giorgio. They were ascribed to Raphael and related to the Città di Castello altarpiece by Valentiner (FFR ; BDIA, 1940–1) and by Venturi

(A, 1940), who also included two other panels, *The Baptism of St Augustine* and *The Dispute of St Augustine*, at that time in the Lazzaroni Collection in Rome. Venturi, however, received no critical support.

13 ⊞ ⊕ 1500 - 01 🗐 ⦂
D. St Nicholas Rescues a Drowning Child Institute of Arts Detroit
The comments in 13C also apply to this work. Volpe attributes the

Preparatory drawing for The Coronation of St Nicholas (13) (Ashmolean Museum, Oxford).

Preparatory drawing for The Coronation of St Nicholas (13) (Musée Wicar, Lille).

execution of this painting to Evangelista da Pian di Meleto.

---

14 ⊞ ⊕ 52×38 1500 - 01 🗐 ⦂
Madonna and Child with a Book (Solly Madonna) Staatliche Museum, Berlin
Formerly in the Solly Collection, it passed to the Kaiser Friedrich Museum in 1821. Unquestionably a Raphael, Gamba and Fischel placed it at the very beginning of the century (1500–1), whereas Gronau dates it slightly later in 1502 ; Venturi in 1502–3 ; and Pittaluga in 1503–4. Conceived in a Peruginesque style and

interpreted with austere simplicity, the brilliance of its colour has probably been lost through extensive cleaning. A copy painted a few months earlier and attributed to Raphael was described by Longhi (PA, 1952).

15 ⊞ ⊕ 34×29 1501-02 ▤ :
Madonna and Child with St Jerome and St Francis
Staatliche Museum Berlin
Formerly in the Borghese Collection, it was sold to the King of Prussia in 1829. It is generally regarded as from the same period as the *Solly Madonna* (14). Extensive restoration has been carried out. Gamba is alone in claiming that the painting should be dated 1499 and that it is based on a drawing by Pinturicchio. Cavalcaselle and Longhi have also recognized an influence from Pinturicchio. They assign a later date to this work, 1501–2. Longi (PA, 1952) reported a copy, attributed to Raphael, formerly in the Grassi Collection in Rome.

16 ⊞ ⊕ 1501-02 ▤ :
Christ Crucified and Saints
Private Collection
A double-sided processional cross formerly in the Visconti Venosta Collection in Rome. Each side of the cross is decorated with four saints. One side shows St Peter at the top, the Virgin and St John the Evangelist at the sides, and Mary Magdalene below. The other side shows St Louis of Toulouse at the top, St Francis and St Claire at the sides, and St Anthony of Padua below. Attributed to Pinturicchio by Ricci (*Pintoricchio*, 1902, 1903, 1915) and by Gamba (D, 1920), who also considered the possibility of Raphael's collaboration. Volpe (PA, 1956), attributes all of the figures to Raphael; 1501–2.

17 ⊞ ⊕ 43×34 1501-02 ▤ :
St Sebastian Accademia Carrara, Bergamo
At one time in the Zurla Collection in Crema; then owned by the engraver Giuseppe Longhi; in 1836 owned by Count Guglielmo Lochis who donated it to the Carrara Academy. Unanimously attributed to Raphael, it is dated 1501–2 by Gamba, Ortolani, Fischel, Longhi, Camesasca and Brizio; 1502–3 by Monti; 1503 by A. Venturi; 1503–4 by Pittaluga; 1503–5 by Gronau and Ottino della Chiesa. The dependence on Perugino confirms the date of 1501–2.

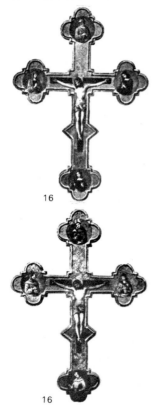

16

16

Preparatory drawings for painting 18 (Ashmolean Museum, Oxford).

18 ⊞ ⊕ 52×44 1501-02 ▤ :
The Resurrection Museo de Arte, São Paulo
The reverse side and frame of this painting bear several inscriptions, the oldest of which, dating possibly from the 16th century, was deciphered as 'Giachino Mignatelli.' Suida (AQ, 1955) believes this to be the name of the first owner. When Bode visited the Kinnaird Collection in Rossie Priory in Scotland, he noticed this painting and informed Cavalcaselle, who never saw the picture which he mentions in his monograph. In 1927 Regteren van Altena linked *The Resurrection* with two drawings in the Ashmolean Museum in Oxford. These drawings had previously been linked with *The Resurrection* which the Church of S. Francesco al Prato in Perugia (12) commissioned Perugino to paint in 1499. Sold in London in 1946 as the work of Mariano di ser Austerio, it came to the São Paulo Museum where Suida identified it with the work mentioned by Cavalcaselle and Regteren van Altena, and revived the attribution to Raphael. In opposition, various critics, including Berenson,

favoured an attribution to Perugino or to the school of Perugino. Supporters of the attribution to Raphael included Ragghianti (SA, 1955), Longhi, Camesasca and Brizio. Suida suggests the date 1502–3; Longhi gives a slightly earlier one, 1501–2. Similarities have been noted between the Kinnaird painting and Perugino's *Resurrection* in the Vatican and one of the panels from the predella of the St Peter Polyptych in the museum at Rouen.

19 ⊞ ⊕ 43,7×34,3 1501-02 ▤ :
An Evangelist and Two Saints Johnson Collection, Philadelphia
Acquired by its present owner in 1909 as a work of Pinturicchio; attributed to Raphael in 1955 by Longhi who identified elements of Pinturicchio and echoes of Melozzo in the figure of the

evangelist; he assigns the date 1501–2 to this work. Volpe (AAM, 1962) agrees with Longhi, as does Camesasca, who has reservations, however, due in part to the condition of the painting. The attribution to Raphael is doubtful.

20 ⊞ ⊕ 1502-03 ▤ :
Scenes from the Life of Enea Piccolomini Libreria Piccolomini, Cathedral of Siena
Vasari, in his life of Raphael, refers, in terms which are not

entirely clear, to Raphael's assisting Pinturicchio in the decoration of the Piccolomini Library. Fischel, Gamba and Longhi are the only critics to accept this information; Fischel and Gamba assign to Raphael two cartoons: *The Meeting of Frederick III with Eleanor of Portugal* (Casa Bedeschi, Perugia) and *The Departure of*

21

22

Piccolomini for the Council of Basel (Uffizi, Florence).

15

17 Pl. I

18

19

Cartoon (20) for The Departure of Enea Piccolomini for the Council of Basel (Uffizi, Florence).

23A

23B

23C

especially in the figures of the four saints, that Vasari stated, 'if his name had not been written on it, no one would have believed it was by Raphael but by Pietro'. The geometric simplification of the composition and the careful relationship between the figures and the spacious, open landscape indicate Raphael's concern to return to the sources which inspired Perugino.

23 ▦ ⊕ 23×41 1502-03 ▤ ⦂

St Jerome Resuscitates Three Men Museu Nacional de Arte Antiga, Lisbon
Panel from the predella of the Mond *Crucifixion*; attributed to Perugino by Passavant who saw the predella in Rome in 1845; considered an early work of Raphael by Cavalcaselle. When Gronau (MFK, 1908) identified this panel and the Richmond *Miracle* with the Mond *Crucifixion*, critical opinion was almost entirely agreed with him (see also 23 A).

23 ▦ ⊕ 23×41 1502-03 ▤ ⦂

St Jerome Performs a Miracle Formerly Cook Collection, Richmond
Similarly identified by Gronau (see 23 B) with the predella of the Mond *Crucifixion*. St Jerome is portrayed holding back the arm of the executioner who is about to behead Bishop Silvanus, while the head of the heretic Sabinian miraculously falls off. Ortolani noted the emphasis given to rhythmic and linear content, which was already evident in the Mond *Crucifixion*. Brizio has pointed out that the two predella panels (23 B and C) are more original than the predella of *The Coronation of the Virgin* in the Vatican (24 A).

21 ▦ ⊕ 1501-03 ▤ ⦂

Cleopatra (?) Private Collection
Regarded by Longhi (PA, 1964) – though by no means universally accepted – as a work of Raphael that can be dated between 1501–3, this painting is part of a series of panels depicting illustrious men and women, originally intended for the Casa Piccolomini. The eleven panels known to be in existence today are scattered among various collections. Numerous artists contributed to this series (Neroccio, Francesco di Giorgio, 'Maestro di Griselda', Gerolamo di Benvenuto, etc.) at the turn of the 15th century. Longhi has identified the subject of the panel as Cleopatra on the basis of the figure's pose, dress and hairstyle.

22 ▦ ⊕ 53×35 1502* ▤ ⦂

Young Man with a Red Beret Uffizi, Florence
Venturi rejected the traditional attribution to Lorenzo di Credi and assigned this portrait first to Perugino and then to Raphael. Salvini (*Catalogo . . . degli Uffizi*, 1952) returns to the attribution to Credi, with reservations, and also refers to Degenhart's attribution to Antonio del Ceraiolo.

The Altarpiece of Città di Castello

23 ▦ ⊕ 279×166 1502-03 ▤ ⦂

The Crucifixion with Two Angels, The Madonna and Sts Jerome, Mary Magdalene, and John the Baptist (Mond *Crucifixion*) National Gallery, London
Painted for the Gavari Chapel in the Church of S. Domenico in Città di Castello, where Vasari and Lazzari (*Vescovi di Città di Castello* 1693) saw it. Later it was purchased by a Frenchman, from whom it was acquired by the Fesch Collection in 1818, and it passed to the collection of Prince Canino in 1845. It belonged to various English collections until 1924 when it was acquired by the Mond Collection. The foot of the cross bears the signature RAPHAEL VRBINAS P; the date 1503 was noted by Margherini Graziani (*L'arte a Città di Castello*, 1897) on an inscription on the altar for which the painting was destined. The predella, which originally accompanied the altarpiece, has been dispersed to different collections (23 B and C). The panel is so strikingly reminiscent of Perugino,

24A

24B

The Oddi Altarpiece

24 ▦ ⊕ 267×163 1502-03 ▤ ⦂

A. Coronation of the Madonna Pinacoteca Vaticana, Rome
Commissioned by Maddalena degli Oddi from Raphael, probably in 1503, for the Church of S. Francesco in Perugia. Requisitioned by the French in 1797, it was taken to Paris where the painting was transferred from panel to canvas. It was returned to Italy in 1815 and placed in the Pinacoteca Vaticana. Ortolani has correctly observed that Raphael, by now thoroughly proficient in the Umbrian tradition, attempted in this work to strengthen the structural composition without, however, resolving the division between the upper and lower sections.

Preparatory drawings (foreground angel-musicians) for 24 A (Oxford, Ashmolean Museum).

Preparatory drawing (apostle at right) for 24 A (British Museum).

Preparatory drawing (apostle at centre) for 24 A (Lille, Musée Wicar).

24 ⊞ ✇ 27×150 1502-03 ▤ ⁝

B. Scenes From the Life of the Madonna
The predella is still attached to the altarpiece and is composed of three panels (each measuring 27 by 50 cm) that have been transferred to a single canvas. Divided and framed by four small pilasters, the panels depict *The Annunciation, The Adoration of the Magi,* and *The Presentation of Jesus in the Temple.* Brizio states that even in his early works Raphael's interest in architecture gives his panels a rhythmical and lucid treatment of space.

Preparatory drawing for The Presentation of 24 B (Oxford, Ashmolean Museum).

Copy after preparatory drawing presumed to be The Annunciation 24 B (London, British Museum).

25 ⊞ ✇ 166×94 1503-04 ▤ ⁝

B. The Creation of Eve
Reverse side of the *Trinity Standard;* see 25 A.

———————————

26 ⊞ ✇ 55×45 1503-04 ▤ ⁝

Portrait of a Man Vaduz, Collection of the Prince of Lichtenstein
On the reverse side of the canvas is written 'Gallery of the Marquis Bovio of Bologna in Santo Stefano Street. Portrait of a duke of Urbino in the early style of Raph. Sanzio of Urbino.' Cavalcaselle first rejected (*History of North Italian Painting,* I), then accepted in 1884 the traditional attribution. He pointed out the characteristics of Francia, to whom he had originally assigned this work. A. Venturi suggests (*Storia . . .,* 1914, VII 3)

25A

Meloni ; whereas Filippini supports Raphael's authorship (CEDA, 1925) allowing, however, for the possible collaboration of Francia. He dates the portrait 1506, the year that Raphael presumably visited Bologna, and identifies the man as Guidobaldo da Montefeltro on the evidence of a letter written by Bembo to Bibbiena in 1516 and of remarks by Baldi (see 57). Filippini's theory was accepted by Gronau who nonetheless considers the portrait a copy.

27 ⊞ ✇ 45×31 1503-04 ▤ ⁝

Portrait of a Man Rome, Galleria Borghese
The picture was listed as by Raphael in the Borghese inventory of 1765 ; the attribution was changed in later inventories to Holbein (from *Fidecommesso . . . Borghese,* 1833). Subsequently, Mündler (in *Cicerone* by Burckhardt, 1869) described it as a self-portrait by Perugino,

while Morelli (ZBK, 1874) returned to the original attribution to Raphael and identified the subject as Pinturicchio. In 1911 Cavenaghi restored the portrait, removing the over-painting (Modigliani, A, 1912). Critical opinion, including Frizzoni (RA, 1912), Ricci (*Pinturicchio,* 1915) and Longhi (*Precisioni . . . 1928*) agreed that the portrait was by Raphael ; A. Venturi disagreed, maintaining that it was by Perugino. The subject has been variously identified as Serafino Aquilano and Francesco Maria della Rovere. The accepted date of execution, 1502–3, was changed by Camesasca to 1503–4, about the time of the *Marriage of the Virgin* Brera.

28 ⊞ ✇ 170×117 1504 ▤ ⁝

The Marriage of the Virgin
Milan, Pinacoteca di Brera
The picture is signed on the architrave of the temple RAPHAEL VRBINAS, and dated on the spandrels MDIIII. Commissioned by the Albizzini

25B

family for the chapel of S. Giuseppe in the Church of S. Francesco in Città di Castello, the painting remained there until 1798 when Napoleon's general Lechi appropriated it. He sold it three years later for 50,000 lire to the dealer Sannazzari who bequeathed it to the Ospedale Maggiore in Milan (1804). Beauharnais purchased it in 1806 and left it to the Academy of Fine Arts in Milan. Restored by Molteni at the end of the 19th century, it was recently restored by Pellicioli when a fanatic damaged it slightly.
The composition is derived from two works by Perugino : *Christ's Charge to Peter* in the Sistine Chapel (1482) and *The Marriage of the Virgin,* painted for the Cathedral of Perugia around 1503–4 and now in the Caen Museum. *Christ's Charge to Peter* sets a group of figures in the foreground against the background of a pizza and an octagonal temple with a triumphal arch at each side. Perugino repeats this motif in simplified form in the Caen *Marriage,* and Raphael takes it

up in his *Marriage of the Virgin.* Raphael probably based his work on the more recent Caen painting rather than on the Vatican fresco which had been painted more than twenty years earlier. In the Perugino, the cupola of the massive temple is cut off by the curve of the picture frame and presses down on the figures. Raphael's spacious and harmonious composition is dominated by a circular rhythm, which is emphasized by increasing the number of sides of the portico

26

from eight to sixteen and by the slender volutes joining the portico to the dome. The important difference between the two works is in the relationship of the architecture to the figures. Raphael's temple rises from a steeper flight of steps and is further from the foreground than is Perugino's. Unlike Perugino, who places his figures in a straight line, Raphael echoes the curve of the temple in his grouping of the figures. The direct precedent for this can be traced, according to Brizio, to the predella of the Vatican *Coronation* particularly in the panels of *The Annunciation* and *The Presentation at the Temple* (24 B). Brizio has noted that Raphael spaces out his figures more skilfully than Perugino. There are preparatory drawings at Oxford, Ashmolean Museum and at London, British Museum. The Brera *Marriage* represents the moment at which Raphael, now twenty years old, is ready to free himself completely from the influence of Perugino.

27

The Trinity Standard

25 ⊞ ✇ 166×94 1503-04 ▤ ⁝

The Trinity with Sts Sebastian and Roch
The Trinity Standard was painted for the Church of the Trinità in Città di Castello. By 1638 it was in poor condition and was taken apart. The two sides of the standard remained in the church until 1867 when Count Della Porta undertook the cleaning and the restoration of the heads of the two saints. The standard subsequently passed to the Pinacoteca Comunale in Città di Castello. A recent restoration brought to light the original surface with its glazing and nuances still intact (Liberti, BICR, 1952). Except for Morelli and Frizzoni, the standard is generally considered to be by Raphael. It probably served as an ex voto at the time of the plague in 1499 in Città di Castello ; hence the usual date of approximately 1500 assigned to this work.

28 Pl. II

29

34

35

transferred to the Staatliche Museum in 1841–2. Formerly attributed to Perugino, today for the most part assigned to Raphael. A.Venturi attributed it to a 'Master of the Diotallevi Madonna', a collaborator of Perugino on the *Madonna della Consolazione* in Perugia (*Storia....*, 1913, VII 2). The traditional dating is 1500–2. Scratched and overcleaned.

32 ⊞ ⊕ diam. 17,9 1504 ▤ ⋮

Madonna of the Book (Connestabile Madonna) Leningrad, The Hermitage
Apparently owned by Alfano di Diamante, uncle of Domenico di Paris Alfani (Memoirs edited by A. Rossi in GEA, VI); later acquired by the Connestabile of Perugia who sold it to the Empress of Russia. Unmistakably a Raphael, dated 1500–2 by Gronau, A.Venturi, Gamba and Fischel; 1504 by Ortolani and Carli. When the painting was transferred onto canvas at the close of the 19th century, it was discovered that the Child was originally playing with a pomegranate, instead of the book, held by the Madonna. Ortolani has noted the unusually beautiful landscape of snow-capped mountains, portrayed with great realism.

33 ⊞ ⊕ 84×55 1504 ▤ ⋮

Madonna and Child (Madonna del Granduca) Florence, Pitti
Owned by the painter Carlo Dolci; purchased in 1799 by Ferdinand III of Hapsburg-Lorraine who so admired the painting that he

took it with him wherever he went. The traditional date is c. 1505. The *Madonna del Granduca* represents one of the earliest and simplest Florentine variations on the theme of the Madonna and Child. Raphael has turned the Virgin slightly to counterbalance the pose of the Child.

34 ⊞ ⊕ 56×48 1504 - 05 ▤ ⋮

The Flagellation Washington D.C., National Gallery of Art
Possibly of Milanese provenance, *The Flagellation*

32

36

belonged to various English collections during the 19th century, the last of which was the Cook Collection of Richmond. In 1948 it was purchased by Samuel H. Kress who gave it to the National Gallery of Washington. Traditionally attributed to Raphael, it was assigned to Spagna by Robinson and to Bachiacca by Borenius (*Catalogo della collezione Cook*, 1913); the latter attribution was supported by Fischel, Gnoli and Van Marle. The attribution to Raphael was renewed by Suida (*Paintings ·... from the Kress Collection*,

1951) and by Longhi (1955) with a date of 1504–5. In Camesasca's *Tutta la pittura di Perugino* (1955), he does not include *The Flagellation* among Perugino's works, but assigns the picture to Raphael, with reservations, and proposes the date of around 1503–4, taking into account the clumsiness of the architectural setting when compared with the Brera *Marriage*. Raphael's authorship appears to be unlikely because the treatment of space is not as mature as, or even similar to, that in Raphael's other works, such as the predella of the Vatican *Coronation* (24 A), from the period 1502–3.

35 ⊞ ⊕ 58×43 1504 - 05 ▤ ⋮

Madonna and Child (The small Cowper Madonna) Washington, D.C., National Gallery of Art
The small Cowper *Madonna* entered the collection of Lord Cowper of Panshanger in 1870 from a private collection in Urbino. The term 'small' is used to distinguish it from another *Madonna*, the large Cowper *Madonna*, also at one time part of Lord Cowper's collection and now also in the National Gallery of Art (82). Before its purchase by the National Gallery, the small Cowper *Madonna* was owned by Duveen (1913) and Joseph Widener. Gamba's date of 1506 is anticipated by one year by Fischel, L.Venturi (*Pitture italiane in America*, 1931) and Suida. Longhi suggests 1504–5. The small Cowper *Madonna*, as A.Venturi observed, is a smaller version of the *Madonna del Granduca* (33).

36 ⊞ ⊕ diam. 87 1504 - 05 ▤ ⋮

Madonna Between Two Saints (Terranuova Madonna) Berlin, Staatliche Museen
Formerly owned by the dukes of Terranuova; in 1855 it passed to its present location. Raphael's authorship has never been contested; 1504–5 is the accepted date. The Terranuova *Madonna* is among the first of the many works painted by Raphael in Florence from 1504–8. The theme of the Virgin and Child (often accompanied by the Infant St John or St Joseph), which Raphael frequently employed in drawings, develops with incredible richness and variations, which reveal Raphael's profound interest in the work of Leonardo. The Terranuova *Madonna* represents one of Leonardo's simplest formulas: the three children (St John, Jesus and unidentified child saint) are dominated by the Madonna, and united by their actions and gazes. The countryside in the background is more detailed and complex than in any earlier Raphael.

29 ⊞ ⊕ 54×39 1504* ▤ ⋮

Portrait of a Young Man Budapest, Szépmuvészeti Museum
Formerly in the Esterhazy Collection, it passed to its present location in 1820 as a work of Luini. It was attributed to Raphael by Viardot (*Les musées de l' Allemagne et de Russie*, 1884), supported by Passavant, Morelli in 1886 and Pulzky (AE, 1896). Contemporary critics generally agree with the attribution to Raphael and assign the date of around 1504. Dissenting opinions have been voiced, mainly by Berenson, Ortolani and Brizio.

30 ▦ ⊕ 1504 c ▤ ⋮

Mary Magdalene and St Catherine Florence, Contini-Bonacossi Collection
Attributed to Raphael by Longhi (PA, 1955) and dated at the beginning of Raphael's Florentine period.

31 ⊞ ⊕ 69×50 1504 ▤ ⋮

Madonna and Child with the Infant St John (Diotallevi Madonna) Berlin, Staatliche Museen
For a long time part of the Diotallevi di Rimini Collection;

31

33 Pl. III

42A

Copy after Raphael (London, British Museum).

37 ⊞ ◷ 17×17 1504-05 ▤⦂

Vision of a Knight London, National Gallery

For a long time in the Borghese Collection in Rome together with *The Three Graces* (38); at the end of the 18th century it passed to England, first to the Ottley Collection, then to other private collections. The subject has been variously interpreted as *Hercules at the Crossroads, Hercules Among the Hesperides* and *The Vision of Scipio.* This last hypothesis was recently strengthened by Chastel (*Art et Humanisme à Florence* . . . 1959) who went back to Silius Italius's poem *Punica* (rediscovered by Poggio Bracciolini in 1417). The young hero, Scipio, who replaces Hercules in Prodico's allegory, is pictured in a typically allegorical situation : confronted with a choice between Venus

37 Pl. IV

38 Pl. V

39

and Pallas, between earthly pleasures and a life of purity. *The Three Graces* has been seen as the sequel of the story : the apples of the Hesperides are given to the triumphant hero by the three Graces as a reward for his virtue. Panofsky first suggested (SBW, 1930) that the two paintings were originally joined to form a diptych. Chastel regards the paintings as an exhortation to youth in honour of Scipione di Tommaso Borghese, born in 1493. *Vision of a Knight* is generally accepted as a Raphael, but there are different opinions on the date of execution. Critics agree that Cavalcaselle's date of 1504 should be changed to 1500-2.

40

38 ⊞ ◷ 17×17 1504-05 ▤⦂

The Three Graces Chantilly, Musée Condé

Formerly in the Borghese Collection in Rome, where it was noted by Manili in *Ville Borghese* in 1650 ; it probably formed one half of a diptych with the *Vision of a Knight* (37). It passed to England early in the 19th century, where it was in various collections until 1885, when it was acquired by the Chantilly Museum. Cavalcaselle relates this work to Federighi's Roman drawing of the three Graces which was sent to Siena in 1502. Suida sees as the source of inspiration the reverse side of a medallion of Niccolò di Forzore Spinelli bearing the inscription *Castitas, Pulchritudo, Amor.* Gronau, Bamba, Fischel and Pittaluga have dated *The Three Graces* between 1498 and 1500 ; A. Venturi in 1501 ;

Cartoon (pricked for the 'transfer') for painting 37 (London, National Gallery).

Ortolani dates it as late as the *Vision* ; Carli in 1504 ; Longhi, supported by the more recent critical studies, in 1504-5.

39 ⊞ ◷ 52×41 1504-05 ▤⦂

Portrait of a Young Man Munich, Alte Pinakothek

Acquired from Dal Riccio of Florence in the 18th century by Ignatius Hugford, who considered it a self-portrait by Raphael ; subsequently in the collections of Count Firmian in Leopoldskron and Ludwig I of Bavaria ; in 1817 it passed to the present collection. Affixed to the reverse side of the painting is a signed statement made by Mengs in 1774 : 'I the undersigned have seen and examined this painting and declare it to be by the hand of Raphael of Urbino . . .' Passavant concurred, whereas Gruyer (*Raphael* . . ., 1881) discounted their attribution, maintaining that the signature RAPHAELLO.VRBINAS FEC.

41

on the buttons of the jacket was false. The Alte Pinakothek stated in the catalogue of 1885 that the artist was an unknown 'Umbro-Bolognese, around 1510'. Cavalcaselle attributed the portrait to Alfani ; Morelli (Lermolieff, *Kunstkritische Studie über . . . die Galerien zu München* . . . 1891) and Berenson (*Italian Pictures of the Renaissance*, 1932) proposed Aspertini. Later catalogues from the Alte Pinakothek state : 'Ferrarese-Bolognese artist, around 1510.' (1936) and 'Bolognese-Umbrian artist around 1505' (1933). Volpe returns (PA, 1956) to the original attribution of a self-portrait by Raphael with the date 1504-5, and reads the signature on the buttons as RAFFAELLO URBINATE. He relates it to the Flemish portraitist Memling because of the columns flanking the subject and the landscape which closely resembles that in Memling's *St John the Baptist in the Desert* (perhaps already in Italy in the Bembo Collection ; now also in the Munich Alte Pinakothek). In its most recent catalogue in 1958 the Alte Pinakothek states : 'Umbrian artist, around 1505. Portrait of a young man, probably Raphael as a young man.' Brizio agrees. The quality of the painting, quite apart from the extensive abrasions and retouching, does not justify the attribution to

42B

42C

42D

42E

42F

42G

Raphael. There are also doubts about the identity of the subject, since there is only a general resemblance to the self-portrait in *The School of Athens* (85 J).

40 ⊞ ◷ 58×36 1504-05 ▤⦂

Portrait of Elisabetta Gonzaga Florence, Uffizi

An inscription on the reverse side of the painting reads : 'Isabella Mantovana, wife of Duke Guido.' The name Isabella appears instead of Elisabetta probably because the duchess,

wife of Guidobaldo da Montefeltro, was accustomed to signing her name Isabetta. Formerly in the ducal collections of Urbino, the portrait passed to the Medici family in 1631 ; in 1925 it was transferred from the Pitti Palace to the Uffizi. First shown as a work of Mantegna, subsequently attributed to Giacomo Francia, Bonsignori (Burckhardt and Cavalcaselle), Caroto (Morelli and Berenson), the early sixteenth-century Veronese school, and

Tamaroccio (Filippini). Durand-Gréville's (RAAM, 1905) attribution to Raphael was discounted by Gronau (RFK, 1907) and A.Venturi (*Storia . . .* 1914, VII 3). In 1925 Gronau (BDA) reversed his opinion and was backed by Longhi, Volpe, Camesasca and Ortolani. Ortolani, however, considered Raphael's authorship 'no more than a general' completion of the portrait which Santi the elder had begun. Brizio and Salvini (*Catalogo . . . degli Uffizi*, 1964), attributed the portrait to the school of Francesco Francia. It is difficult to consider this a work of Raphael because of the rigidly frontal pose, which is antiquated and awkward in comparison with Raphael's Florentine works. The quality was judged by Ortolani as 'deficient' and the posture is very close to Francia. A date of around 1504–5 can be assigned to the picture, since the duchess was born in 1471.

41 ⊞ ⊕ 42,5 × 28,5 / 1504 - 05 ▤ ⫶

Portrait of Emilia Pia da Montefeltro Baltimore, Epstein Collection
On the reverse side is written 'Emilia Pia da Montefeltro,' accompanied by a seal deciphered as: 'Fontico tedescho di Venezia.' The painting probably passed from the collections of the dukes of Urbino to the Medicis of Florence about the middle of the 17th century, then to Vienna where it was cleaned by Sikora before it was acquired by the Covay-Stoop di Erlenbach Collection in Zurich. It subsequently passed to the Kleinberger Gallery in New York and finally to the Epstein Collection. The subject was identified by Dennistoun (*Memoirs of the Dukes of Urbino*, 1909) and is confirmed by the resemblance to a medallion attributed to Adriano Fiorentino by Fabriczy (JPK, 1903). Gronau (BDA, 1925) attributed the portrait to Raphael and was followed by Berenson, Longhi, Volpe and Camesasca; Brizio, however, disagreed. The picture is close to the *Elisabetta Gonzaga* in the Uffizi and is equally unlikely to be by Raphael (see 40).

The Colonna Altarpiece

42 ⊞ ⊕ 30 × 68 / 1503 - 05 ▤ ⫶

A. God the Father Between Two Angels New York, Metropolitan Museum
See 42 B.

42 ⊞ ⊕ 68 × 68 / 1503 - 05 ▤ ⫶

B. Madonna Enthroned with Five Saints New York, Metropolitan Museum
The saints to the left are Peter and Catherine; to the right, these are the Infant St John being blessed by Jesus, Margaret (or Cecilia) and Paul. Raphael was commissioned to paint the altarpiece by the Sisters of S. Antonio in Perugia,

who expressly requested that the Christ Child should appear clothed (Vasari). The Sisters were granted permission in 1677 to sell the painting; Antonio Bigazzini of Perugia purchased this, the central panel of the altarpiece, and the lunette (42 A). The two panels passed subsequently to the Colonna collection in Rome and to that of Francis I, King of the Two Sicilies, after which they were transferred by Francis II to Spain in 1861. In 1901 they were purchased by Pierpont Morgan, who bequeathed them to the New York Metropolitan Museum. The predella was purchased from the Sisters by Christina of Sweden in 1663; it passed through various collections until it was sold as part of the Orléans Collection in 1789 and disappeared. Panels can be found in Dulwich, New York, Boston and London (42 C to G). The altarpiece has been assigned to the year 1504 by Fischel and Suida, 1504–5 by Ortolani; 1505 by Berenson and Carli. The majority of critics, however, agree with Cavalcaselle's theory – which has been sustained by Gronau, L.Venturi (*Pitture italiane in America,* 1931), Longhi and Camesasca – that the work was begun before Raphael moved to Florence in the autumn of 1504 and completed during one or two of his visits to Umbria, so that the execution spans a period of approximately two years, 1503–5. Brizio favours the idea of a protracted execution, but suggests that Raphael first undertook the altarpiece at the

43

44

45

beginning of his Florentine period.

42 ⊞ ⊕ 24 × 16 / 1503 - 05 ▤ ⫶

C. A Franciscan Saint Dulwich College Gallery
A piece of the same height and four centimetres wide was added to the right side of this painting. It is generally regarded as the left pilaster of the Colonna altarpiece (see 42 B), not by the hand of Raphael (Berenson). It is in a poor state of preservation due to repainting.

Preparatory drawing for 42 E (New York, Morgan Library).

42 ⊞ ⊕ 24 × 16 / 1503 - 05 ▤ ⫶

D. St Anthony of Padua Dulwich College Gallery
Companion piece of the *Franciscan Saint* (see 42 C) with a similar addition, in this case on the left side. Similarly in poor, if not worse, condition.

42 ⊞ ⊕ 24 × 28 / 1505* ▤ ⫶

E. The Agony in the Garden New York, Metropolitan Museum
This part of the altarpiece was probably on the left of the dismembered predella (see 42 B); it formerly belonged to various English private collections. Although Cavalcaselle maintained that it was by one of Raphael's assistants, contemporary opinion considers it autograph. Repainting has been carried out on the upper sections.

46A

46B

42 ⊞ ⊕ 24 × 28 / 1505* ▤ ⫶

F. Pietà Boston, Isabella Stewart Gardner Museum
Formerly in various European collections; in 1909 acquired by the Isabella Stewart Gardner Museum. Originally, it was probably placed to the right of *The Procession to Calvary* (42 G). Unanimously attributed to Raphael

42 ⊞ ⊕ 23 × 85 / 1505* ▤ ⫶

G. The Procession to Calvary London, National Gallery
Central panel of the predella of the Colonna altarpiece (see 42 B). Acquired by the National Gallery in 1913 from the collection of Lord Windsor. It is basically autograph, although certain critics, Cavalcaselle, Berenson, etc., believe that Raphael was assisted.

_____

43 ⊞ ⊕ 26 × 87 / 1504? ▤ ⫶

St Francis Dresden, Gemäldegalerie
Generally assigned to Perugino attributed to Raphael by A. Venturi (*Studi dal vero . . .,* 1927) who considered it a panel from the dismembered predella of the Colonna altarpiece.

Venturi reaffirmed his theory in the monograph *Raffaello,* 1952, revised by his son Lionello, who did not, however, include this work among the parts of the Colonna altarpiece, enumerated in his *Pitture italiane in America* in 1931.

44 ⊞ ⊕ 333 × 218 / 1505 ▤ ⫶

The Deposition Florence, Galleria dell'Accademia
Filippino Lippi was commissioned in 1500 by the Church of the Annunziata in Florence to paint *The Deposition*. When Lippi died on 15 April, 1504, the unfinished painting was entrusted to Perugino for completion. Perugino availed himself of an assistant whom A. Venturi believes was Andrea d'Assisi and Gamba believes was Raphael. Neither of these two hypotheses has been accepted.

45 ⊞ ⊕ 47 × 35 / 1505 ▤ ⫶

Young Man with an Apple Florence, Uffizi
As part of the Della Rovere collections, it passed from the dukes of Urbino in 1631 to the Medici collections, first to the Pitti Palace, then to the Uffizi. The attribution to Raphael was advanced by Durand-Gréville (RAAM, 1905), who received almost unanimous critical support. A.Venturi (*Storia . . .,*

93

1914, VII 3) attributed the portrait to the school of Francia, and Filippini (CEDA, 1925) attributed it to Tamaroccio. Durand-Gréville also identified the subject as Francesco Maria della Rovere. In attributing the work to Francia, critics refer specifically to the exceptional radiance of the colours. The sureness of the composition has been used as an argument in favour of Raphael's authorship. The Flemish influence, common to other works by Raphael of this same period, suggests a date of c. 1505.

The Ansidei Altarpiece

46 ⊞ ⊕ 274 × 152 / 1504 - 06 ▤ ⦙

A. Madonna and Child Enthroned Between Two Saints London, National Gallery
The saints are St John the Baptist and St Nicholas of Bari. Commissioned for the Ansidei Chapel in the Church of S. Fiorenzo dei Serviti in Perugia, the altarpiece was purchased in 1764 by Lord Spencer, who replaced it with a copy of Nicola Monti. It was subsequently owned by the Duke of Marlborough, from whom it was acquired by the

47

National Gallery in 1885. Only one panel (46 B) from the dismembered predella is known. On the upper part of the throne is written SALVE MATER CHRISTI; below the Virgin's left hand, on the edge of her cloak, is the date which, because of abrasions, has been variously interpreted: MDV by Passavant and Waagen (*Art Treasures in Great Britain*, 1854); MDVI by Cavalcaselle; and even MDVII by other critics. The composition of the altar is undoubtedly Peruginesque, yet Raphael has made important changes. The architectural setting is reduced to a large luminous archway, against which the figures are placed

Preparatory drawing for 49 (Florence, Uffizi).

with a strong sense of balance and with greater monumentality than is usual in Perugino's work.

48

46 ⊞ ⊕ 26 × 53,3 / 1504 - 06 ▤ ⦙

B. St John The Baptist Preaching London, Mersey Collection
This is the only predella panel of the Ansidei altarpiece to have survived. Its provenance follows the same course as that of 46 A up to the year 1764; later it passed into the Lansdowne Collection and finally to its present home. The predella was originally accompanied by two other panels depicting *The Marriage of the Virgin* and *The Miracle of St Nicholas,* which were presumably placed under corresponding saints in the main part of the altarpiece.

47 ⊞ ⊕ 1505 ▤ ⦙

St Martin and the Beggar Private Collection
The sides and lower portion of this painting have probably been cut off; attributed to Raphael by Volpe (AAM, 1962), but not accepted by modern critics.

48 ⊞ ⊕ 31 × 27 / 1505 ▤ ⦙

St Michael and the Dragon Paris, Louvre
Mentioned with the *St George* (49) in a sonnet by Lomazzo who relates that it was sold by a Milanese to Count Ascanio Sforza of Piacenza; it subsequently passed to the collections of Cardinal Mazarin, Louis XIV and finally the Louvre. There are various opinions regarding the date. Fischel: 1500; A.Venturi: 1501; Gronau: 1500–2; Suida: 1502; Gamba, Rosenberg, Ortolani, Carli: 1504; Camesasca and Brizio: 1505. The identical sizes and the similarity of the figure types suggest that the *St Michael* and *St George* were both executed around 1505. The monsters in the background are reminiscent of Bosch.

50

49 ⊞ ⊕ 31 × 27 / 1505 ▤ ⦙

St George and the Dragon Paris, Louvre
In 1895 Cartwright (*The Early Work of Raphael*) referring to two inventories (1542 and 1547) from the reign of Henry VIII of England, argued that, contrary to the traditional assumption, it was not the Washington D.C. *St George*, but the Louvre *St George*, which was presented as a gift to the King of England by Guidobaldo da Montefeltro on the occasion of the conferment upon the latter of the Order of the Garter. Cartwright, followed by MacCurdy (*Raphael Santi,* 1917), points out that each inventory contains two entries describing paintings of St George. While the second of these descriptions does not apply to either of the two works by Raphael, the first could apply to the Louvre *St George,* but definitely not to the one in Washington: 'a painting with the figure of St George, his lance

broken and his sword in hand.' Both the Washington and Louvre catalogues, from Ricci (*Description . . . du Louvre,* 1913) to Bazin (*Trésors . . . au Louvre,* 1951) have ignored Cartwright's theory. The subject was discussed recently by Lynch (GBA, 1962), who found a mention of the Louvre *St George* and the *St Michael* (48) in a sonnet by Lomazzo (*Rime,* 1587) in which he tells of an avaricious and ignorant Milanese who is reproved for

49

51 P. VII

having sold the two works to Count Ascanio Sforza of Piacenza. The paintings must have gone first to Piacenza before passing to Cardinal Mazarin's collection where they were documented in 1661. The painting listed in the English inventories of 1542 and 1547 disappeared from Chair House, the king's study at Westminster, before November 1550. The *St George* and *St Michael* passed from Mazarin's collection to the royal house of France and finally to the Louvre. Lynch rightly holds that both versions of the *St George* were executed by Raphael for Guidobaldo da Montefeltro who probably kept one for himself and sent the other to England with Castiglione who, because of illness, did not leave Urbino before July 1506. The Louvre *St George,* painted around 1505, is more dramatic than its successor.

50 ⊞ ✦ 28×22 1505-06 ▤ ⫶

St George and the Dragon
Washington D.C., National Gallery of Art
It is generally believed that this work was executed for Guidobaldo da Montefeltro, who received the Order of the Garter from Henry VIII of England. St George is wearing a garter on his left leg with an inscription in gold HONNI, the first word of the motto of the Order of the Garter. There is some disagreement concerning which of the two St George's was sent with Castiglione by the duke to the King of England (see 49). The painting was acquired by the Earl of Pembroke at the beginning of the 17th century and was then sold to Ewrard Jabach acting for Cardinal Mazarin. It was sold in turn by Mazarin, who also owned the Louvre *St George*, which he retained. The

52

53

Washington *St George* remained in France until the 18th century when it was purchased by Catherine of Russia ; subsequently in the Hermitage, it was sold by the Soviet Government in 1937 to the Andrew Mellon Collection and is now in the National Gallery of Art. The accepted date of execution, 1505-6, is questioned only by Fischel and Suida who propose a date of c. 1504-5. Cavalcaselle regards the Washington version as being inspired by Donatello's relief in Or San Michele in Florence.

51 ⊞ ✦ 65×51 1505-06 ▤ ⫶

Portrait of a Young Woman (Lady with a Unicorn) Rome, Galleria Borghese
This portrait, depicting St Catherine before its restoration in 1935, was attributed to Perugino in the Borghese inventory of 1760 ; to Ridolfo

del Ghirlandaio by Morelli (ZBK, 1874) ; to Granucci by Morelli and Berenson ; to Andrea del Sarto, with reservations, by A.Venturi in 1893. In 1916 Cantalamessa (BDA) noted that the cloak, the hands, the wheel and the crown (symbols of St Catherine's martyrdom) were the work of a different artist from the one who did the rest of the painting. Longhi (VA, 1927 ; P, 1928 ; *Precisioni...*, 1928) supported Cantalamessa's findings and attributed the work to Raphael. However, some modern critics doubt this attribution. Its restoration in 1935, which followed an X-ray photograph, revealed the original appearance of the work, which contained a unicorn, symbol of chastity, in the lap of the woman, and a more ample landscape in the background. The portrait may have been repainted because of damage, especially to the landscape and the unicorn. Ortolani suggests that the subject is the 'real' Maddalena Doni (56) on the basis of comparisons with a drawing in the Louvre. This theory has had no critical support because of the considerable difference in size and composition between this work and the portrait of Agnolo Doni (55).

52 ⊞ ✦ 66×52 1505-06 ▤ °°

Portrait of a Woman (La Gravida) Florence, Pitti
Catalogued as the work of an unknown painter by the Pitti in the early 18th century, it was attributed to Raphael by Masselli (*Galleria Pitti...*, 1839). Cavalcaselle, the only critic to disagree, attributed the painting to Ridolfo del Ghirlandaio. The date varies from between 1505 and 1506. Filippini's identification (CEDA, 1925) of the subject as Emilia Pia da Montefeltro has not been accepted. Brizio called attention to the richness of the colours and the especial Raphaelesque 'tone' which is to be found, not in the general atmosphere of the painting, but rather in the merging of the various planes in the portrait, which thus acquires great naturalness and clarity.

53 ⊞ ✦ 30×25 1506 ▤ ⫶

Christ Blessing Brescia, Pinacoteca Tosio Martinengo
The painting passed from the

54

55 Pl. VI

Mosca di Pesaro Collection to Count Tosio di Brescia in 1832. Cavalcaselle dates it 1504 pointing out its Florentine influences. 1502 is the date assigned by Fischel ; 1502–3 by Gronau ; 1503 by A.Venturi and Ortolani.

54 ▦ ✦ 45×33 1506 ▤ ⫶

Self-Portrait Florence, Uffizi
Perhaps formerly in Urbino ; brought to the Accademia di San Luca in Rome by Federico Zuccari in 1588 ; subsequently it passed to the collection of Cardinal Leopoldo de' Medici. The traditional attribution to Raphael, with the approximate date of 1506, has been frequently doubted by recent scholars. The extremely poor state of preservation prevents reliable attribution.

55 ⊞ ✦ 63×45 1506 ▤

Portrait of Agnolo Doni Firenze, Pitti
Companion to the portrait of Mȧddalena Strozzi who married Agnolo Doni in 1503 ; both works remained in the family until 1826 when they were acquired by Leopold II, Grand Duke of Tuscany. Both portraits can be dated around 1506. The superb assurance and monumentality of the pose are set off by the emphasis on expressive interpretation, which gives life and reality to the study, and by the highly refined treatment of colour of both subject and background. On the reverse is a monochrome by a later follower of Raphael illustrating the deluge sent by Zeus, an episode from the myth of Deucalion and Pyrrha.

56 ⊞ ✦ 63×45 1506 ▤

Portrait of Maddalena Doni Florence, Pitti
The provenance of this portrait is the same as that of Agnolo Doni (55). Although the pose is reminiscent of Leonardo's *Mona*

Lisa, now in the Louvre, the subject has been rendered without any of the mystery of Leonardo's portrait. Maddalena Doni seems to be almost physically present, thanks to the ample forms of her sumptuous dress. On the reverse, the artist, whose work appears on the back of the Agnolo Doni portrait, has illustrated in monochrome another episode from Deucalion and Pyrrha showing their rescue from the deluge.

57 ▦ ✦ 69×52 1506 ▤ ⫶

Portrait of Guidobaldo da Montefeltro Florence, Uffizi
The provenance of this work is the same as that of the portrait of Elisabetta Gonzaga (40). This panel has also been attributed to Giacomo Francia, Bonsignori, Caroto, etc. In Bembo's letter to Bibbiena of 19 April, 1516, it is not certain whether his reference to 'our Duke' applies to Guidobaldo or to Giuliano de' Medici. Durand-Gréville (RAAM, 1905) was the first to attribute this work to Raphael and was followed by other critics, including Gronau, Longhi, Volpe (PA, 1956) and Camesasca. Salvini's attribution (*Galleria degli Uffizi*, 1964) to the school of Francia reaffirms A.Venturi's earlier theory. As with 40, it is too stiff and mechanical to be by Raphael.

57

56

58 ⊞ ✦ 1506? ▤ °°

Portrait of Bembo
Around 1530 Michiel saw in Bembo's house in Padua a portrait of Pietro Bembo 'by the hand of Raphael'. This lost work was probably painted in 1506 during Bembo's stay in Urbino.

59 ⊞ ✦ 1506? ▤ °°

The Agony In The Garden
According to Vasari, painted for Guidobaldo da Montefeltro ; subsequently given by Leonora, wife of Francesco Maria della Rovere, to Paolo Giustiniani and Pietro Quirini, monks of the Camaldolese order. Alippi (RBAI, 1915) published letters which demonstrated that Elisabetta, wife of Guidobaldo, gave the portrait to the monk Michele da Firenze. The Camaldolese monks presented it to Guidobaldo II in 1570. In a letter from Bembo dated 6 May, 1506, from Urbino, he refers to the portrait passing to 'don Michele' of Florence who had withdrawn into the Camaldolese monastery. Passavant mentions it in the Fuller Maitland Collection in Stanstead, after which there is no further trace of the picture.

60 ⊞ ✦ 29×21 1506 ▤ ⫶

Madonna (The Orléans Madonna) Chantilly, Musée Condé
Commonly identified with one of the two small Madonnas that Vasari saw in the possession of the Duke of Urbino and claims were painted for Guidobaldo da Montefeltro by Raphael during a visit to Urbino. It is in all probability the work listed in the inventory of the ducal palace as a 'small painting on wood of a Madonna holding Christ in her arms by Raphael.' It then passed to the Orléans family and in 1869 to the Duke of Aumale and finally to its present location. Passavant's hypothesis that the background was repainted by a disciple of Teniers was rejected by Cavalcaselle.

95

Vasari's date of 1507 was accepted until recently; contemporary critics prefer the date 1506 or 1505 (Fischel); in perfect condition.

61 74×57 1506

Madonna With The Beardless St Joseph
Leningrad, The Hermitage
This could be one of the two works which Vasari mentioned as painted by Raphael in Urbino for Guidobaldo da Montefeltro. No information about its provenance is available until the 18th century, at which

60

61

time the painting belonged to the Duke of Angoulême in Paris. It was cleaned by Vendine and then passed to the famous Crozat Collection and finally to the Hermitage. Generally dated round 1506; Gamba and Fischel, on the other hand, date it approximately 1505. The faces reveal traces of restoration.

62 diam. 101,4 1506

Holy Family With the Palm
London, Ellesmere Collection
Milanesi claims that this might be the second of the two paintings noted by Vasari as executed by Raphael in Florence for Taddeo Taddei. Nothing certain is known about this work before the 17th century when it belonged to the Countess Chiverni in Paris. It passed to the Orléans Collection in 1792 and subsequently to the Ellesmere Collection. The dates suggested vary between 1505 and 1507. Since it is close to the *Madonna del Prato*, it must have been painted around 1506. Important restorations have been made to conceal two vertical cracks. Cavalcaselle believes that the landscape recalls Lake Trasimene.

62

63 113×88 1506

Madonna and Child With The Infant St John (Madonna del Prato, or Madonna del Belvedere)
Vienna, Kunsthistorisches Museum
On the hem of the Virgin's gown is the date M.D.VI. This is generally regarded as one of the paintings executed by Raphael in Florence for Taddeo Taddei, whose heirs invited Vasari to view these two works. The *Madonna* passed from the Taddei to Ferdinand of Austria (Baldinucci, *Notizie...* 1681) who kept it in his residence in Innsbruck until 1663 when it was transferred to his castle of Ambras in the Tyrol. In 1773 it was acquired by the imperial Viennese collections where it took the name *Madonna del Belvedere*. The three figures form a pyramid. Although inspired by Leonardo's cartoon of *The Virgin and Child with St Anne*, which he displayed in the Church of the Ss. Annunziata, Raphael's work lacks the mystery of Leonardo's picture. Behind the figures the broad landscape is cut by the misty band of a lake, which, like 62, has been identified by Cavalcaselle as Lake Trasimene near Passignano.

64 185,5×152,5 1507

Madonna Between St Jerome and St Francis
London, National Gallery
Perugino was commissioned in June 1507 to paint this work for the Church of Sta Maria Nuova dei Servi in Perugia and probably completed it in September of the same year. The painting was acquired by the Della Penna family in 1821 and

Detail of 64 (centre part).

subsequently by the National Gallery in 1879. A. Venturi remarked on the lack of stylistic similarity with works of Perugino from that same period and suggested the collaboration of Andrea d'Assisi. In 1955

64

Longhi, supported by Camesasca, maintained that the composition of Perugino had been largely executed by Raphael. Comparisons with works of Raphael of that same period do not confirm this theory.

65 38×19 1507*

St John Bergamo, Accademia Carrara
Both this and the following work

are traditionally attributed to Mariotto Albertinelli.

66 38×19 1507*

Mary Magdalene Bergamo, Accademia Carrara
See 65.

67 66×37 1507*

Madonna (Northbrook Madonna) London, Northbrook Collection
Attributed to Raphael by Venturi, whereas Gronau supported Cavalcaselle's attribution to Spagna. A. Venturi's opinion was accepted by Ortolani and recent criticism. The date varies: 1505–6

65

66

63

Preparatory drawing for 68 (Oxford, Ashmolean Museum).

according to Longhi and Camesasca; 1507 according to Brizio; 1508 according to Ortolani.

68 107×77 1507

Madonna And Child With The Infant St John (Madonna of the Goldfinch)
Florence, Uffizi
Painted in Florence for

Preparatory drawing for 69, La Belle Jardinière (Paris, Louvre).

Lorenzo Nasi around 1507; Vasari mentions that it was damaged when Nasi's house collapsed on 9 August, 1548. Milanesi alters this date to 12 November, 1547. The *Madonna* was subsequently restored, according to Gamba, by Michele di Ridolfo del Ghirlandaio. It passed to its present location in 1666 with the collection of Cardinal Carlo de' Medici. The pyramidical composition, which

67

68 Pl. XII

Raphael used in numerous paintings of the Florentine period, is simplified here, with a resulting accentuation of the masses, and is modelled by an intense chiaroscuro. The painting marks the apex of Raphael's search for monumentality. There are old copies in the Victoria and Albert Museum in London, in the sacristy of Vallombrosa and in a private collection.

69 ⊞ ✦ 122×80 1507 📖 ⋮

Madonna And Child With The Infant St John (La Belle Jardinière) Paris, Louvre
The name *Belle Jardinière* is derived from the beauty of the Madonna seated in the meadow. On the hem of her cloak, above her foot, is the signature RAPHAELLO VRB. and near her elbow is the date MDVII. Passavant and Clement read the date as 1508 claiming that the terminal mark is the remains of a third Roman numeral I. A reference by Vasari has led to the identification of the painting as a work executed for Filippo Sergardi of Siena, which was left unfinished by Raphael and was completed after his departure by Ridolfo del Ghirlandaio, who added a piece of blue drapery. This is, however, unlikely to refer to the present picture. The painting was purchased in Sienna on behalf of François I of France. This stylistically complex work is derived from both Leonardo and Michelangelo.

The Baglioni Altarpiece

70 ⊞ ✦ 81,5×88,5 1507? 📖 ⋮

A. God The Father And Angels Perugia, Galleria Nazionale dell'Umbria
The lunette from *The Deposition* (see 70 B) ; formerly regarded as a seventeenth-century copy (Marchesi, *Principali monumenti . . . di Perugia*, 1857). Berenson believed that at least part could be attributed to Raphael ; according to Gnoli, Domenico Alfani executed the painting from drawings by Raphael. Not generally considered a work of Raphael, it does, however, derive from Raphael's drawing now at the Musée Wicar, Lille. Camesasca has brought to light a work of approximately the same dimensions (formerly in Lucca) probably painted around the middle of the 16th century, which he claimed to be closer to the original composition.

69 Pl. XIII

70 ⊞ ✦ 184×176 1507 📖 ⋮

B. The Entombment of Christ (Borghese Deposition) Rome, Galleria Borghese
Signed and dated RAPHAEL VRBINAS M.D.VII.
Commissioned by Atalanta Baglioni in memory of her son Grifonetto who was killed in the course of a violent family

Preliminary study for 70 B (Oxford, Ashmolean Museum) showing like the two drawings below, an early stage which was subsequently abandoned.

dispute over the control of Perugia in July 1500. *The Entombment* with the lunette and predella (see 70 C) remained in the family chapel in the church of S. Francesco al Prato in Perugia until 1608 when it was secretly sent to Rome to Pope Paul V who gave it to his nephew Cardinal Scipione Borghese. In answer to the townspeople's objections, the pope merely ordered a copy to be executed by Cavalier d'Arpino. From 1797 to 1815 the painting was requisitioned by the French. The development of the composition can be followed through the sixteen preparatory drawings divided among the Ashmolean Museum in Oxford, the British Museum, the Louvre and the Uffizi, which have been analyzed by Fischel. Raphael altered his original plan for a *Lamentation* in favour of an *Entombment*. Analysis of the preparatory drawings shows the development towards this final version to be perfectly logical. Great emphasis is given to the contrasting figures of the bearers, the numerous classical and Michelangelesque motifs (notable in the dead Christ and the kneeling Mary whose form, twisted around to support the Virgin, is derived from the Madonna of the Doni Tondo), and the enamel-like colours,

70 A

Sixteenth-century copy of what is presumed to be the original, 70 A; (formerly in a private collection, Lucca).

70B Pls. VIII-IX

which create a sense of plasticity and sculptural monumentality. In spite of the beauty of the landscape and of the intensity of the expressions, it can be argued that Raphael does not achieve a compositional unity in this his first large dramatic picture.

70 ⊞ ✦ 1507 📖 ⋮

C. The Theological Virtues Rome, Pinacoteca Vaticana
Same history as *The Entombment* (70 B). It is composed of three panels (each 16 × 44 cm.) unanimously attributed to Raphael. The three Virtues, portrayed on medallions, are painted in a delicate grisaille ; each of the Virtues — Faith, Hope and Charity — is flanked either by two putti or two little angels.

70C Pl. X

Preparatory sketch (Col. 2) for 70 B and a copy after a lost drawing for the picture (both in London, British Museum).

97

71 Pl. XIV

72 Pl. XI

73

71 ⊞ ⊕ 29×21 / 1507

Holy Family With The Lamb
Madrid, Prado
Formerly in the Falconieri
Collection in Rome, it was
acquired by the Escorial
probably in the 18th century and
passed to the Prado in 1837. On
the neckband of the Virgin's
gown is written RAPHAEL.
VRBINAS. MDVII. The date has
also been read as 1505 and
1506; currently, however, the
preferred date is 1507. A
number of old copies are known.

Preparatory drawing for 73
(Vienna, Albertina).

72 ⊞ ⊕ 132×98 / 1507

**Holy Family With St
Elizabeth and The Infant
St John (Canigiani Holy
Family)** Munich, Alte
Pinakothek
RAPHAEL. VRBINAS is written
on the border of the Virgin's
gown. Vasari saw this work in
Florence in the house of
Domenico Canigiani's heirs,
from whom it passed to the
Medici. It was subsequently
included in the dowry of Anna
Maria Luisa, daughter of Grand
Duke Cosimo III, for her
marriage to the Elector, Prince
William of The Palatinate; later
it went to the Düsseldorf gallery
and in 1801 was transferred to
Munich to escape the French.
The date is generally given as
1507 or 1508 (Gamba).
Overpainting done in the 18th
century was removed from the
upper section at the end of the
19th century. Von Reber
(*Catalogue de la
Pinacothèque . . . de Munich*,
1885) maintained that
originally there was a group of
angels above (they are shown in
an old copy in the Corsini
Gallery) which was later
removed along with a strip of
the canvas and then partially
covered over while the
painting was in Düsseldorf.
Raphael's variations on the
pyramid become increasingly
more complex as he includes
more figures and searches for
stronger rhythms to link the
figures. The composition recalls
the extent of Raphael's debt to
Michelangelo (in the figure of
St Joseph) and to Leonardo
during his stay in Florence. An
old copy is preserved in the
Galleria Nazionale in Urbino.

74 Pl. XXIV

73 ⊞ ⊕ 81×56 / 1507*

**Madonna (Bridgewater
Madonna)** London, Ellesmere
Collection
At one time part of the
Serguelay and Orléans
collections; in 1792 it passed to
the Ellesmere Collection. The
date fluctuates between 1506
and 1507. Several drawings (in
the Albertina in Vienna and the
British Museum in London) for

this work reveal in Raphael's
search for movement a profound
assimilation of Leonardo 's
principles. In good condition,
despite the transfer from wood
to canvas.

75

77

74 ⊞ ⊕ 64×48 / 1507

**Portrait of A Woman (La
Muta)** Urbino, Galleria
Nazionale delle Marche
It passed from the Uffizi in
Florence to its present location
in 1927. The traditional
attribution to Raphael was
rejected by Rumohr (*Italienische
Forschungen, III*), by
Cavalcaselle, Morelli (1897),
Rosenberg and Berenson, who
also abandoned his
long-standing attribution to
Perugino in 1953. A. Venturi,
however, returned to the theory
of Raphael's authorship
Attempts to
identify the subject as a
Strozzi or Elisabetta Gonzaga
(Filippini, CEDA, 1925), have
met with no critical support.

75 ⊞ ⊕ 37×40,5 / 1507

Portrait of A Young Man
Hampton Court, Royal Gallery
Passavant, who saw the
painting in the Kensington
gallery, read the inscription
RAFFAELLO URBINAS FEC
on the clasps of the jacket and
related the work to a painting
catalogued in the collection of
James II as a self-portrait of
Raphael. This attribution was
disputed by Gruyer who
considered the signature false,
and by Cavalcaselle who
maintained that the painting
was 'executed with great care'
by a Florentine assistant of
Raphael and identified the

structure in the right background
as the tomb of Cecilia Metella.
The portrait was later designated
as 'Umbrian school' in the
catalogues of Hampton Court
and the exhibition of the king's
pictures (London, 1946–7).
Raphael's authorship was,

79

however, reaffirmed by Volpe
(PA, 1956) who believes this
work might very well be a self-
portrait executed around 1507.
In poor condition, the portrait
may have been cut off at the
bottom.

76 ⊞ ⊕ 1507?

**The Adoration of the
Shepherds**
Mentioned as *The Adoration of
the Shepherds* in a letter to
Francia dated 5 September,
1508; but the letter is not
generally considered authentic.
Two works on the same subject
are mentioned by Malvasia
(*Felsina Pittrice*, 1678) in
Bologna: one in Palazzo
Bentivoglio, before the fire of
1506; the other in the house of
Fantuzzi. Filippini (CDA, 1925)
believes that this work, executed
during Raphael's supposed stay

in Bologna, is the one seen by
Oretti in Fantuzzi's house
(around 1770) and described as
a small manger scene.

77 ⊞ ⊕ 77,5×56,5 / 1507*

**Madonna (Colonna
Madonna)** Berlin, Staatliche
Museen
Identified by Rumohr as the
Madonna which, according to
Vasari, was begun by Raphael
and completed by Ridolfo del
Ghirlandaio.
Vasari's reference has also been
associated with *La Belle
Jardinière* (69). Formerly in the
Salviati Collection in Florence
and the Colonna Collection, it
was acquired by the Prussian
government. Raphael's
authorship is accepted by most
critics.

78 ⊞ ⊕ 1507–08?

Madonna
In a letter to his uncle Ciarla
dated 2 April, 1508, Raphael

Preparatory drawings of the Madonna and St Bruno for 79 (Paris,
École des Beaux-Arts; Florence, Uffizi).

80

81

refs to an altar painted for the wife of Giovanni della Rovere, prefect of Rome. Nothing else is known about this *Madonna*.

79 ⊞ ⊘ 276×224 1507-08 ▤ ⋮
Madonna Enthroned With Four Saints and Four Angels (Madonna of the Baldacchino) Florence, Pitti
The saints portrayed on the left are St Peter and St Bruno; on the right St James and St Augustine. Begun around 1507 for the Chapel of the Dei family in the Church of Santo Spirito in Florence, it was left unfinished when Raphael departed for Rome in 1508. Until the 16th century it was preserved in the parish church of Pescia. In 1697, it was acquired by Prince Ferdinando de' Medici who had it restored and certain parts completed by the brothers Niccolò and Agostino Cassana (Richa, *Notizie . . . delle chiese fiorentine*, 1754). At this time a strip was added to the top making it the same size as another painting next to it. The contribution of the Cassana brothers is of limited value and easily distinguished from the rest of the work. The Madonna remained in the Pitti except for the period 1799–1813 when it was removed to Paris by the French.

Gamba refuted the traditional attribution to Fra Bartolommeo in favour of one to Raphael. Raphael initially pursued a course similar to that of the older Fra Bartolommeo, but soon surpassed him with complex compositions which inspired his Florentine contemporaries and Lorenzo Lotto.

80 ⊞ ⊘ base 389 1507-08 ▤ ⋮
The Trinity And Saints Perugia, Church of the Monastery of S. Severo
At the top of the fresco, the figures of God the Father and the putto on the right have almost entirely disappeared. In the centre Christ is seated between two angels with the dove of the Holy Ghost above Him; on His left are the saints Maurus, Placidus and Benedict; on His right are Romuald, Benedict the Martyr and John the Martyr. In 1521 Perugino frescoed the six standing saints. On a screed at the base of the wall to the left is written : RAPHAEL DE VRBINO D. OCTAVI/ANO STEPHANI VOLTERRANO PRIO/RE SANCTAM TRINITATEM ANGE/LOS ASTANTES SANCTOSQUE/ PINXIT/A.D. MDV
The grandiose semicircular composition, evoking motifs from Fra Bartolommeo's *Last Judgment*, contains the initial inspiration for *The Disputà* (85). In a poor state of preservation.

81 ⊞ ⊘ 29×21,5 1508 ▤ ⋮
Madonna And Child With The Infant St John (Esterhazy Madonna) Budapest, Szépmüvészeti Museum
A note attached to the back states that the painting was presented by Pope Clement XI to the Empress Elisabeth who in turn gave it to Prince Kaunitz; upon his death it passed to the Esterhazy family. Cavalcaselle remarked on the difference between this landscape with its classical ruins (similar to those of the Temple of Vespasian in Rome) in the left background and the landscape of the preparatory drawing in the Uffizi. His dating of this work at

82

the beginning of Raphael's Roman period was sustained by Gronau, Gamba, Ortolani, Suida and Brizio. A different dating, around 1505–7, is proposed by A. Venturi, Fischel, Longhi and Camasasca. Berenson rightly judged this an unfinished work.

82 ⊞ ⊘ 68×46 1508 ▤ ⋮
Madonna (Large Cowper Madonna, Niccolini Madonna) Washington D.C., National Gallery of Art
On the neckband of the Virgin's gown is written MDVIII/R. V. PIN. Formerly in the Niccolini

Collection in Florence, it passed to the Cowper Collection in 1780. In 1937 it was acquired by Mellon who bequeathed it to the National Gallery. Slight damage can be seen, as, for example, in the disappearance of the clouds; partially restored.

83 ⊞ ⊘ 77×53 1508 ▤ ⋮
Madonna (Tempi Madonna) Munich, Alte Pinakothek
Noted by Cinelli (*Bellezze di Firenze*, 1677) in the house of the Tempi; acquired by Ludwig I of Bavaria in 1829. This is one of Raphael's most successful works, which can be dated approximately to the end of his Florentine period. The painting is dominated by a single spiral movement. The monumental rhythm of the figures is set against the simplified landscape. Cavalcaselle mentions a copy belonging to G.A. Sogliani in Rome with the date MDX and the initials R.S. of which the R is damaged.

84 ⊞ ⊘ 71×53 1508 ▤ ⋮
St Catherine of Alexandria London, National Gallery
A picture by Raphael of St Catherine is mentioned in a letter of August 1550 written to Agosto d'Adda by Aretino who relates that he sent the painting to Venice. It is not possible to identify this picture as the St Catherine in the National Gallery, which can first be traced in the 18th century in the Aldobrandini and Borghese collections in Rome. Purchased by Alexander Day, probably around 1795, it was shown in London in 1801. It subsequently belonged to William Beckford, who bequeathed it to the National Gallery in 1839. Unquestionably a Raphael, the traditional dating (1506–7) is altered by Hendy to 1508 (*The*

Preparatory drawing for 81 (Florence, Uffizi).

National Gallery, 1960), at the end of Raphael's Florentine stay. Instead of employing all of the usual symbols of St Catherine – the crown, the sword and the book – Raphael uses only the wheel against which the saint is leaning. This follows the spiral motif of the mantle and arms and the slow turning of the mass of the body. The majestic proportions of St Catherine, which are set against the misty background, assume even greater plasticity through the enamel quality of the colour. St Catherine's pose is a prelude to the great Roman altarpieces.

Preparatory drawing for 84 (Louvre, Paris).

83

84

99

The Stanze

The new apartments chosen for Julius II, who was unwilling to accept the ground floor rooms decorated by Pinturicchio for Alexander VI Borgia, are located in the Vatican on the upper storey of the Palace of Nicholas III in the north wing which was partly reconstructed by Nicholas V. Proceeding from west to east these are : the Stanza dell'Incendio, the Stanza della Segnatura, the Stanza di Eliodoro, the Sala di Costantino. The first three stanze have cross-vaulted ceilings and measure approximately ten metres by eight ; the fourth stanza : ten metres by fifteen. According to Vasari, before Julius commissioned Raphael, certain walls had already been frescoed by Piero della Francesca, Luca Signorelli and Fra Bartolommeo della Gatta. The new decorations had been given initially to a group of artists which included Sodoma, Peruzzi, Bramante and Lotto. It is not possible to establish the exact date of Raphael's arrival in Rome, but Vasari says that he left Florence suddenly on the invitation of the pope who had been advised by Bramante. Raphael did not leave Florence before April 1508 as is shown by a letter to his uncle Simone Ciarla on 21 April of that same year. Since

the authenticity of the letter to Francia of 5 September, 1508, is highly questionable, the first reliable information on Raphael's presence in Rome is an order for payment issued on 13 January, 1509 by the pontifical treasury *ad bonum computum picturae camerae . . . testudinatae*, which presumably refers to the Stanza della Segnatura. Raphael's Vatican undertakings must therefore have commenced some time before the end of 1508. On seeing Raphael's first efforts, the pope did not hesitate to dismiss the other painters and destroy the scenes they had done (Vasari).

Stanza della Segnatura

The decoration of Julius II's apartments began with the Stanza della Segnatura in which the cycle begun in 1508 was completed in 1511, as is shown by the inscriptions in the *Parnassus* fresco and on the architrave of the window beneath the lunette of the *Virtues*. During this same period Michelangelo was decorating the ceiling of the Sistine Chapel, the first part of which was unveiled in August of 1511. The name Segnatura comes from the fact that the

Stanza was destined to be the seat of the tribunal of the Segnatura Gratiae. The generally accepted hypothesis, first set forth by Wickhoff (JPK, 1893), that the Stanza was originally intended as the pope's library, was rejected by Klaczho (RDM, 1894) and by Chastel, who pointed out that the representation of the doctrines of humanism, with its divisions of theology, philosophy, poetry and jurisprudence was not in fact applicable to the decoration of a library. Recently the hypothesis that the Stanza was a library has been revived. The Christian-Platonic concepts that provided the inspiration for Raphael's figures have been studied at great length, notably by Hettner (*Italienische Studien*, 1879), by Redig de Campos (IV, 1938), by Hoogewerff (RPAA, 1947–9) and by Chastel, maintains that only by grossly under estimating the originality and the philosophical and technological significance of the Renaissance could certain critics have been led to associate these concepts strictly with scholastic ideas. In the Stanza della Segnatura the wisdom of the learned is not degraded but placed alongside of the Word of God ; Poetry is placed among the higher powers of the spirit ; Justice ceases to be one of the cardinal virtues

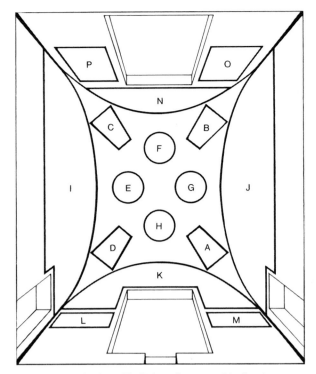

Plan in perspective (seen ideally from the centre of the floor) showing the frescoes of the Stanza della Segnatura (85); the letters refer to the Catalogue of Works.

and is placed, as Plato would have it, at the summit of the moral hierarchy. Harmony reigns between the ancient world and Christianity. The theme of the cycle is the glorification of the ideas of Truth, Goodness and Beauty : Truth in its two aspects of theology – revealed truth – (*The Disputà*) and in its natural or rational form of philosophy (*The School of Athens*) ; Goodness in the cardinal and theological virtues and in Law, both religious (*Gregory IX Approves the Decretals*) and civil (*Tribonianus Presents the Pandects to Justinian*) ; Beauty is represented by Poetry (*Parnassus*). In these frescoes Raphael has portrayed well-known historical figures who not only convey a symbolic meaning but have precisely individualized features and gestures. On the ceiling, in direct relationship with the scenes below, are the personifications of the same principles of Truth (theological and philosophical), Goodness and Beauty. It is not certain who conceived of this complex *speculum doctrinale*, but there is no reason to reject the information of Paolo Giovio that the plans for the decorations were laid out *ad praescriptum Julii Pontificis* (*Vita Raphaëlis*). It would be unjust to consider Raphael a mere transposer of someone else's ideas, however sublime. He accepted suggestions for subject matter without allowing himself to be restricted, indeed, in his frescoes he gave form and life to these ideas before they had been intellectually formulated. The preparatory drawings for *The Disputà* show the way in which Raphael changed his programme. Raphael's supreme position as an artist in

relation to the papal court is proven by the undisputed admiration and immense prestige he enjoyed among the literati of the epoch. The frescoes of the Stanza della Segnatura evolved from a series of preparatory drawings which were the fruit of much elaboration and meditation on what was at first undoubtedly a broad and undefined theme. After the completion of the ceiling, part of which had been executed previous to Raphael's arrival, the decoration continued with the wall of *The Disputà* followed by *Parnassus, The School of Athens* and the *Virtues*. Originally the plinth was covered with wooden panelling (as in the Sala del Cambio in Perugia and the Studiolo in the place at Urbino) decorated with inlays by Fra Giovanni da Verona, who began work in 1508, and with chiaroscuri by Perino del Vaga at the time of Paul III.

The ceiling

Cornices painted with grotesques divide the area into thirteen sections. Around an octagonal centre, with putti bearing the papal arms, are four medallions, corresponding to the lunettes of the walls, with personifications of Theology, Justice, Philosophy and Poetry. Four rectangular-shaped scenes in the pendentives depict *Adam and Eve, The Judgment of Solomon, The First Motion* (or *Astronomy*), and *Apollo and Marsyas*. Inserted between the octagon and the rectangles are smaller scenes, each with two stories ; one above, in monochrome, with a historical subject taken from Livy, the other, below, in polychrome, with a mythological theme derived from Hyginus. In the

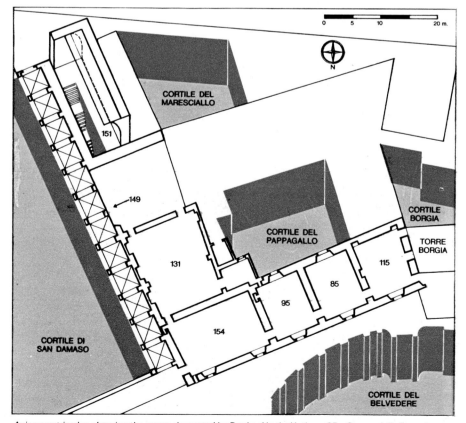

Axionometric plan showing the rooms decorated by Raphael in the Vatican. 85 – Stanza della Segnatura; 95 – Stanza di Eliodoro; 115 – Stanza dell'Incendio di Borgo; 131 – Sala dei Palafrenieri; 149 – The Logge; 151 – The Loggetta; 154 – Sala di Costantino.

85 A

85 B

85 C Pl. XV

85 D

top of the arches. The putti carry emblems by which they can be recognized as genii of the elements. The genie of the air is placed above *The Disputà* while the genie of fire is above *Parnassus*. According to Chastel, this proves that changes were made as the work progressed, thereby excluding the possibility that Raphael devised the subdivisions of the ceiling. Only the four medallions and the scenes in the pendentives are believed to be by Raphael. The other parts, including the cornice grotesques, were executed by Raphael's predecessor, whom most critics identify as Sodoma (considered by Coppier as the author of the whole ceiling). A. Venturi ascribes the central octagon to Bramantino. The ceiling can be dated at the end of 1508, since most critics believe it was the first fresco to be carried out.

85 ⊞ ⊕ '120 × 105' 1508 ☰ ⫶
A. The First Motion or Astronomy
This has been variously interpreted as an allegory of the beginning of the universe, with Philosophy studying the globe of the cosmos, or as Astronomy contemplating the universe.

85 ⊞ ⊕ '120 × 105' 1508 ☰ ⫶
B. The Judgment of Solomon
The influence of classical sculpture can be noted, for example, in the figure of the executioner which is derived from one of the Dioscuri on the Quirinal in Rome.

85 ⊞ ⊕ '120 × 105' 1508 ☰ ⫶
C. Adam and Eve
Both classical and Leonardesque reminiscences are evident in the figure of Eve. Arslan (D, 1929) has attributed this panel to Sodoma.

85 ⊞ ⊕ '120 × 105' 1508 ☰ ⫶
D. Apollo and Marsyas
Florentine Neoplatonists attributed a precise symbolic value to the story of Apollo and Marsyas in reviving a Pythagorean motif which also appears in Dante (Paradise, I 19 & 21): the victory of divine harmony over the anguished soul of terrestrial passions. The panel has been attributed to Peruzzi by Redig de Campos and to Sodoma by Arslan.

85 ⊞ ⊕ diam. 180' 1508 ☰ ⫶
E. Theology
The female figure, wearing a white veil, green cloak and red dress (the colours of the theological virtues) is flanked by putti bearing tablets inscribed with *Divina (rum) re (um) notitia*, taken from Justinian (Wauscher). According to Fischel (*Raphaels Zeichnungen*, V, 1925) the preliminary drawing shows that Theology was represented by Beatrice.

larger scenes the figures appear raised up against a background of simulated gold mosaic. The decoration of the ceiling was conceived as one subject and is directly related to the scenes on the walls below: above *The Disputà* is *Theology* followed by *Adam and Eve* on the right; above *The Virtues* is *Justice* followed by *The Judgment of Solomon*; above *The School of Athens* is *Philosophy* followed by *The First Motion*; above *Parnassus* is *Poetry* followed by *Apollo and Marsyas*. The smaller double scenes are intended to signify the agreement of the elements with the four disciplines portrayed in the medallions: *Justice* and earth, *Philosophy* and water, *Poetry* and air, *Theology* and fire. These relationships are taken up again in different combinations in the putti at the

Preparatory drawing for the putto on the right in 85 E (Lille, Musée Wicar).

Preliminary sketch for the central figure in 85 E (Oxford, Ashmolean Museum).

85 ⊞ ⊕ diam. 180' 1508 ☰ ⫶
F. Justice
The female figure holds the scales and the sword. Two putti on each side hold tablets on which is written *Ius suum unicuique tribuit*, from Justinian.

85 ⊞ ⊕ diam. 180' 1508 ☰ ⫶
G. Philosophy
The female figure, wearing a blue, red, green and yellow gown, the colours of the four elements, is seated on a throne on each side of which is a figure of Artemis of Ephesus, symbol of nature's fecundity.

85 E

85 F

Philosophy is holding two volumes entitled *Moralis* and *Naturalis*, and the two genii are holding tablets inscribed with *Causarum cognito*, from Cicero.

85 ⊞ ⊕ diam. 180' 1508 ☰ ⫶
H. Poetry
Poetry, crowned with laurels and wings spread wide, holds the lyre and a book. The two putti hold tablets inscribed *Numine afflatur*, from Virgil (*Aeneid*, VI 50)

The wall frescoes

85 ⊞ ⊕ base 770' 1509 ☰ ⫶
I. The Disputà
The name given to this fresco comes from a seventeenth-century interpretation of a passage from Vasari. The fresco shows the fathers of the Church, The Trinity, God the Father and Christ, involved in a *Disputà* on the consecrated Host raised up to heaven in the monstrance above the altar. The mystery of the Eucharist, the pre-eminent miracle binding heaven and earth, is contemplated by the Church Triumphant and the Church Militant, represented respectively by an assembly of prophets, apostles and saints,

Preparatory drawing for the central figure in 85 H (Windsor, Royal Library).

85 G

85 H

and by a council of doctors of the Church, popes and the faithful. The two groups are arranged in two superimposed concentric semicircles around a central axis which unites the Host and the Trinity. At the apex of the lunette is God the Father blessing, between two groups of angels. Lower down a large halo frames Christ, the Virgin and St John the Baptist. Seated to the left of the three central figures on a bank of clouds are St Peter, Adam, St John the Evangelist, David, St Stephen and Jeremiah; to the right; Judas Maccabeus, St Lawrence, Moses, St Matthew (according to some, St James Major or St James Minor), Abraham and St Paul. Only some of the terrestrial figures are identifiable, among whom are, on the left, Fra Angelico in a Dominican habit; Bramante leaning against the balustrade as he turns to talk to an unidentified person; Francesco Maria della Rovere, the young man who turns to the viewer while pointing to the altar; Gregory the Great, saint and pope, who has the features of Julius II, seated with the book *Liber Moralium* at his feet; St James, the old man reading next to the lion. To the right of the altar, next to St Ambrose, the seated bishop looking upward, is St Augustine; behind him are St Thomas Aquinas, Pope Innocent III and St Bonaventure. Dressed in a golden cope with the tract *De Sanguine Christi* at his feet, Sixtus IV stands on the first step; behind him is Dante. Further back, partially hidden by a dark hood, is Savonarola. The extreme simplicity of the structure and composition of this fresco illustrates the theme with absolute immediacy and geometric clarity. The single figures are rigorously subordinated to the whole in their symmetrical grouping. The variety of the poses and of the movements of the figures are unified by the common motivation of adoration. *The Disputà* thus becomes a visible manifestation of the *civitas Dei* composed of the Church's divine and earthly founders. The huge marble block in the right background seems to allude to both the corner-stone and the reconstruction of St Peter's (Grimm, *Ausätze zur Kunst*, 1915). There is a recollection of Raphael's Umbrian style in the great fan-shaped rays raised in stucco that descend from the lunette amid a host of angel's heads. The grouping of the figures re-echoes Fra Bartolommeo's *Last Judgment*, but with a new grandeur. Pure Leonardesque elements are evident in certain figures (such as the young man who is possibly Francesco Maria della Rovere) and in the ornamental knot motif on the altar frontal. The opening of the door on the right is perfectly integrated into the composition and is harmoniously balanced on the left by the balustrade on which Bramante is leaning. *The Disputà* is unanimously attributed to Raphael, except

for the presumed figure of Francesco Maria della Rovere which Arslan (D, 1929) regards as the work of Sodoma.

Preliminary sketch for the figures to the left of the altar in 85 I (London, British Museum).

in the fresco. The cartoon lacks the architecture but this seems to be indicated by the treatment of perspective (Beltrami, *Il cartone di Raffaello . . .*, 1920). Vasari affirms that the architecture was designed by Bramante. A more acceptable theory is that Raphael was directly inspired by Bramante's ideas to achieve a monumental architecture which is a grandiose and heroic frame for the figures. Identifiable figures in the fresco are : Socrates, to the left of the two central figures, conversing with a group of young men among whom are Alcibiades (or Alexander) in armour. Xenophon and Aeschines (or Alcibiades) ; on the extreme lower left is Zeno with a baby holding a book which Epicurus, crowned with vineleaves, is reading. Pythagoras is seated further to the right in the foreground, making notes in a large book while Telange (?) holds a tablet for him ; leaning over Pythagoras' shoulder is Averrhoës who is wearing a white turban. Heraclitus rests his elbow on a large block ; Diogenes is stretched out on the steps ; the man standing next to Heraclitus, pointing to an open book which rests on his knee, has been variously identified as Parmenides, Xenocrates and Aristossenus. In the right foreground Euclid, surrounded by his disciples, bends over to measure a geometric figure with a compass ; behind him is Zoroaster holding a globe of the heavens and Ptolemy,

completion of the fresco, as revealed by the joints of the plaster. The ponderous form and the intense modelling of the philosopher, who has been given the features of Michelangelo, indicate that Raphael wished to pay homage to Michelangelo by rendering him in his own style. The artists portrayed in *The School of Athens* thus become part of the higher assembly of the learned, and the plastic arts, formerly classified as mechanical, are raised to the same level as the liberal arts. *The School of Athens* has also been interpreted as a representation of the seven liberal arts (Springer ; Chastel) : in the left foreground, grammar, arithmetic and music ; on the right, geometry and astronomy ; at the top of the stairs, rhetoric and dialectics. The two groups in the foreground symbolize the science of numbers in its two aspects, musical and astronomical. The tablet supported by the young man at the feet of Pythagoras bears symbolic references to systems of musical harmonies also reproduced by the

85 ⊞ ⊕ base 770* 1509 - 10 ▤ ⦂
J. The School of Athens

Opposite *The Disputà*, which glorifies revealed Truth, is *The School of Athens*, celebrating the rational search for truth. The figures of the ancient philosophers and the learned are placed within an edifice of solemn and grandiose proportions with motifs from Roman architecture of the late Imperial period which is probably inspired by Bramante's plans for the new St Peter's. The subject of the fresco is still controversial, and the programme not really known. In the niches on each side of the first great arch are statues of Apollo and Minerva, both of which were directly inspired by classical prototypes. The significance of the two statues is explained in the bas-reliefs located below them : a struggle between nude male figures and a Triton who is carrying off a Nereid symbolizes the violence and lust which dominate the ignoble side of the human soul and must be commanded by reason, represented by Apollo. The allegory under Minerva is more difficult to decipher, but seems to symbolize the intellect governed by divine powers (Hettner). Other niches with statues and bas-reliefs can be seen from the side along the walls of the nave. The medallions on the spandrels of the cupola depict a man looking

Study for the figure of Christ in 85 I (Lille, Musée Wicar).

First draft for the upper group in 85 I (Oxford, Ashmolean Museum): composition is still close to 80.

First draft for the lower group in 85 I (Chantilly, Musée Condé): the breadth of the final work is missing from this sketch.

up from a book and a woman resting her arm on a globe of the universe. Their actions appear to repeat those of the two central figures standing at the top of the stairs : Plato, holding the *Timaeus*, points upward to the heavens and Aristotle, holding the *Ethics*, stretches his arm out with the palm of his hand turned down toward the earth. In the gestures of the two philosophers Raphael has expressed the essence of their doctrines, demonstrating his unique ability to sum up the most complex ideas in simple, concrete images. Vasari apparently refers to this talent — which must have seemed miraculous to Raphael's contemporaries — when he wrote 'he composed these stories with such ease and rapidity that they vied with the efficacy of the written word.' The nucleus of the composition, the two figures of Plato and Aristotle, are framed against the background of the sky by the last arch. The Ambrosiana cartoon in Milan approaches the final composition of the fresco. The chiaroscuro effects of the cartoon, which echo the style of Leonardo, are not, however, so accentuated

mistakenly crowned as a king of Egypt, holding a globe of the earth. This evocation of the temple of wisdom through illustrious men of the past is closely linked to the present in a series of portraits of famous contemporaries. The wise men who fill the Bramantesque basilica are portraits of artists, humanists and princes of the papal court : Plato has the features of Leonardo ; Heraclitus is Michelangelo ; Euclid is Bramante ; the young man who represents Epicurus is Federico Gonzaga ; the young man dressed in white behind Pythagoras' group is Francesco Maria della Rovere ; Zoroaster is perhaps Pietro Bembo ; Raphael himself is portrayed on the far right, next to Sodoma, as the young man with a black beret. Heraclitus, who does not appear in the Ambrosiana cartoon, was inserted after the

theologian Zarlino (*Istituzioni armoniche*, 1558). Chastel suggests that the finger of Plato expresses the final orientation : from the science of numbers to music ; from music to cosmic harmony, and thence to the divine order of ideas. Other critics emphasize the Christian content. The fresco is regarded by critics as an autograph work executed, with the exception of the figure of Heraclitus, in late 1509 and into 1510. Coppier

Sketch for 85 I (Montpellier, Musée Fabre).

85 J Pls. XX-XXV

Study for a muse in 85 K (London, Colville Collection).

Studies for the figure of Apollo in 85 K (Lille, Musée Wicar).

alone has attributed the whole lunette to Sodoma except for the portrait of Raphael which he recognizes as by Raphael himself. Redig de Campos (AF, 1945) has interpreted the golden markings on the collar of Euclid's tunic as the letters RVSM, Raphaël Urbinas Sua Manu. Calosso (ibid.) proposed extending the reading of the markings to include the following letters ; his interpretation reads, *Raphaël Urbinas* MDVIIII. Redig de Campos rejects this last theory.

Urania on the right behind Erato. The eighteen poets surrounding Apollo have been identified as : in the left foreground, Alcaeus, Corinna, Petrarch, Anacreon and Sappho, holding a screed with her own name on it. Ennius listens rapturously to Homer, while Dante, between them but further back, watches Virgil who turns toward him, Statius at his side. On the right, descending the hill, is Tebaldeo (or Castiglione or, according to a recent hypothesis of Tolnay,

on the slopes. The pseudo-antique musical instruments of the engraving are replaced in the fresco : Calliope, Erato and Sappho hold instruments which have been meticulously copied from the sarcophagus of the Muses in the Museo delle Terme (Winternitz, RPAA, 1952–4) ; Apollo is playing a modern lyre – almost as if to point out the extra-historical value of the mythical figure (Chastel) – fitted with nine chords, instead of the usual seven, in keeping

with the number of muses. Raphael's interest in classical antiquity was gradually becoming more precise and archeological in accordance with the orientation of the humanists. By his use of classical motifs which establish a subtle parallel between the classical and modern poets, Raphael, as Brizio so aptly notes, 'with supreme naturalness, has made incarnate the linguistic program proclaimed by the Humanists themselves, namely, to give richness and dignity to the vernacular by means of quotations from the Latin tongue.' Compared with the other frescoes of this Stanza, *Parnassus* has a pronounced rhetorical character. On the embrasure of the window is written : JVLIVS. II. LIGVR. PONT. MAX. ANN. CHRIST. MDXI. PONTIFICAT. SVI. VIII.

Preliminary sketch for the figure of Dante in 85 K (Windsor, Royal Library).

The cartoon for 85 J; note the absence of the figure of Heraclitus, which was inserted after the completion of the fresco (Milan, Pinacoteca Ambrosiana).

Studies for 85 K (Windsor, Royal Library).

Study for 85 K (Oxford, Ashmolean Museum).

85 ⊞ ⊕ base 670* 1510-11 ▤ ⦙
K. Parnassus
The fresco extends to the areas on each side of the window, which measures 305 cm. at its base. At the top of the hill, near the spring, Castalia, Apollo is playing the lyre ; at his side are Calliope and Erato who are presiding over the chorus of the other muses : Thalia, Clio and Euterpe on the left behind Calliope ; Polyhymnia, Melpomene, Terpsichore and

Michelangelo), Boccaccio, Tibullus, Ariosto (or Tebaldeo), Propertius, Ovid and Sannazzaro. In the right foreground is seated Horace. The identification of the various poets has never been firmly established. Chastel maintains that precise relationships must be found between the nine muses, the nine ancient poets and the nine 'modern' poets, in addition to groupings according to poetic genres. On the other hand, the classical poets of *Parnassus* are probably portraits of Raphael's humanist contemporaries. The original project, to which Raimondi's engraving corresponds and which Vasari describes instead of the fresco, portrays Apollo and the muses in a dark forest of laurels on the summit of a hill with a swarm of angels in flight bearing crowns destined for the poets grouped

85 K Pls. XXVI-XXVII

103

85 L

85 M

tower in the left background. In the 18th century it belonged to the Orléans Collection and subsequently to the son of the historian Mackintosh; it was bequeathed to its present home in 1906. The painting was severely damaged when it was transferred from panel to canvas, thus preventing an accurate appraisal. Attritubted to Raphael by Cavalcaselle with the agreement of some critics; generally dated around 1508–9; Camesasca assigns it to the year 1512.

The date 1511 can be applied to the conclusion of the decoration of the whole Stanza. The fresco was probably begun in 1509; retouching is evident in the area of the sky. The attribution to Raphael has been rejected by only one critic, Coppier, who favours Sodoma. There is some damage, which is not serious.

85 ⊞ ✛ base 185 1514 ▤ ⋮

L. Augustus Prevents the Executors of Virgil's Will From Burning The Aeneid
See remarks in 85 M.

85 ⊞ ✛ base 660* 1511 ▤ ⋮

N. The Virtues
Opposite *Parnassus* is the lunette showing *The Virtues*. Three female figures seated on the plinth represent, from left to right, Fortitude, wearing a helmet, and holding an oak branch, alluding to the family name of Julius II; Prudence, in a green and white gown, and Temperance, holding the reins. The fourth cardinal virtue, Justice, dominates the group from the medallion on the ceiling, in accordance with Plato's doctrines, though contrary to St Augustine's, that Justice ranks first among the virtues. Five putti unite the three figures with harmonious movements. Three of the putti symbolize the theological virtues: the putto picking fruit from the branch held by Fortitude is Charity; the putto in the centre holding the torch, Hope; the one pointing to the sky, Faith. The proportions of the figures and the impressive composition reveal Michelangelo's influence which has been assimilated into a classically composed rhythm. On the architrave of the window below is the inscription:

damage has affected much of the detail. Some critics attribute the execution to Raphael's collaborators; for example, Coppier assigns it to Sodoma. However, it is now commonly agreed that Raphael executed the fresco. Pallucchini (*Sebastian Viniziano*, 1944) has cautiously advanced the theory that Sebastiano del Piombo carried out the restorations to which Dolce refers (*Dialogo della Pittura*, 1557).

85 ⊞ ✛ base 220* 1511 ▤ ⋮

P. Gregory IX Approves The Decretals
Placed on the side of *The Disputà*, this celebrates ecclesiastical law. The figure of the pope is a portrait of Julius II; the cardinal on the left holding the cope has the features of Giovanni de' Medici; the other two cardinals on the left have been identified as Alessandro Farnese and Antonio Del Monte. The fresco is in a poor state of preservation. The fact that Julius II is portrayed with a beard would suggest a dating at the end of 1511: the pope left Rome without a beard (he later vowed

85 O

85 N Pls. XXVIII-XXX

85 ⊞ ✛ base 180 1514 ▤ ⋮

M. Alexander The Great In The Act of Depositing The Books Of Homer In The Tomb of Achilles
Raphael's authorship of this work and the preceding one (85L) is questionable. Cavalcaselle considers them stylistically worthy of Raphael, but probably executed by Perino del Vaga. Fischel is the only critic to disagree and regards these as works of Raphael. They were probably done after the other frescoes of the Stanza, according to Suida, in 1514.

JVLIVS. II. LIGVR. PONT. MAX. AN. CHRIS. MDXI. PONTIFICAT. SVI. VIII. Cavalcaselle maintained, on the basis of stylistic similarities with the Stanza di Eliodoro, that the frescoes of this wall were the last in the room to be executed.

85 ⊞ ✛ base 220* 1511 ▤ ⋮

O. Tribonianus Presents the Pandects to Justinian
Placed on one side of *The School of Athens*, this celebrates natural law. Serious

not to shave until he had liberated Italy) and returned to Rome that same month. This representation of the pope, given particular prominence, indicates how the theme of the decoration of the Stanza changed around 1511 to the glorification of the papacy.

86 ⊞ ✛ 76,5×63 1509* ▤ ⋮

Madonna (Madonna of the Tower) London, National Gallery
The name by which this work is usually known derives from the

85 P

87 ⊞ ⊕ 38×33 1510 ▤ ⦂

Madonna and Child With the Infant St John (Aldobrandini Madonna, Garvagh Madonna) London, National Gallery
The background probably represents the environs of Rome (Cavalcaselle). From the Aldobrandini family, the *Madonna* passed to the Borghese Collection; acquired at the end of the 18th century by Day, it was brought to England where it became part of Lord Garvagh's Collection (1818).

86

87

88 Pl. XXXV

88 ⊞ ⊕ 79×62 1510-11 ▤ ⦂

Portrait of A Cardinal
Madrid, Prado
Attempts to identify the subject have included the following suggestions, none of them convincing: Giulio de' Medici, Bibbiena, Innocenzo Cybo, Alidosi, Scaramuzza-Trivulzio and Ippolito d'Este. It was considered a late work of Raphael, until A. Venturi dated it around 1510–11. The extreme naturalness and elegance of the pose, the sureness and simplicity of the composition, the very subtle colouristic contrasts make this one of Raphael's finest portraits. Some restoration is evident, especially at the bottom.

89 Pl. LI

89 ⊞ ⊕ 68×44 1510-11 ▤ ⦂

Madonna and Sleeping Child With The Infant St John (Madonna of the Diadem) Paris, Louvre
The ownership of this painting cannot be documented before 1620, when it was part of the La Vrillière Collection in Paris. It subsequently belonged to the Prince of Carignan (1728) and to Louis XV of France (1743). Cavalcaselle has pointed out the collaboration of Penni, to whom Fischel attributes the entire execution. The conception of the work is Raphael's, but he had no hand in its execution. In a poor state of preservation. The dating varies between 1510 and 1512; only Filippini assigns it to the year 1507.

90 ⊞ ⊕ diam. 98 1511 ▤ ⦂

Madonna And Child And The Infant St John (Alba Madonna) Washington D.C., National Gallery of Art
We know from a manuscript by Resta (Milan, Biblioteca Ambrosiana) that this work remained in the Church of the Olivetani in Nocera until the 17th. century. It was then acquired by the Marchese del Carpio, viceroy of Naples, who took it to Spain, where in 1793 it is mentioned by Conca (*Descrizione odeporica . . .*) as belonging to the Duke of Alba in Madrid. In 1836 it was purchased by Nicholas I of Russia and later by Mellon, who bequeathed it to its present home. Originally painted on panel it is generally dated around 1511, although Gronau proposes the date 1508–10.

91 ⊞ ⊕ 220×160 1511? ▤ ⦂

St Luke Paints the Madonna and Child Rome, Accademia di San Luca
First mentioned in 1579 in the Accademia di San Luca, to whom the painting was bequeathed, according to Baglione, by Federico Zuccari. Passavant maintains that it was given by Pietro da Cortona to the Church of SS. Luca e Martino and transferred to the Accademia by order of Sixtus V. The president of the Accademia, Antiveduto Grammatica, allegedly sold the original, substituting a copy. Transferred to canvas in 1857 by Pileri; in 1949–51 Vermehren undertook the removal of the over-painting by Scipione Pulzone; in 1956 it was restored by

Cellini who attributed it to Raphael (BDA, 1958) and dated it late 1511, when the second Stanza was begun. The traditional attribution to Raphael, which has been rejected by Cavalcaselle, Müntz, Berenson, Ricci, Sartorio and Camesasca, is unacceptable after the recent restoration. According to Cavalcaselle and Cellini, the young man behind St Luke might be a self-portrait of Raphael.

92 ⊞ ⊕ 295×225 1511 ▤ ⦂

Galatea Rome, Farnesina
The theme of the fresco, which occurs in Theocritus and Ovid, may be taken from Politian. It was painted by Raphael under a lunette by Sebastiano del Piombo, in the room 'of the Galatea' on the ground floor of the villa of Agostino Chigi, probably in 1511. A description which may refer to this fresco is given in the *De Viridario Augustini Chigi . . . libellus* by Gallo, published in Rome that same year. Galatea, whose features and pose recall the London *St Catherine* (84), rides the waves triumphantly on a shell pulled by a pair of dolphins and led by the young boy Palaemon. She is accompanied by a cortege of Tritons and Nereids, while putti shoot arrows from the sky. The crystalline light emphasizes the powerful bodies of the Tritons against the exquisite mosaic of the background: the marble-green of the unfurrowed surface of the sea and the intense Pompeian red of Galatea's cloak blown, like her hair, by the wind which fills the veil of

90 Pl. XXXVI

91

the nearby Nereid. The unreal colours suggest Raphael's knowledge of ancient Roman painting. Cavalcaselle relates this work to the bas-relief of the Chorus of Aphrodite (Musei Capitolini) and, despite the lack of documentation, attributes a large portion of the execution to Giulio Romano. Hartt (*Giulio Romano*, 1958) rejected this hypothesis. The quality of the work, in spite of damage and 17th-century retouching, and the note of archeological and mythical classicism, indicate that this is entirely autograph.

93 ⊞ ⊕ 250×155 1511-12 ▤ ⦂

The Prophet Isaiah Rome, Church of S. Agostino
On the third pilaster to the left of the nave the prophet is portrayed enthroned between two putti who hold a plaque with a dedication in Greek: 'To Saint Anne, Mother of the Virgin, to the Holy Virgin, Mother of God, to Jesus the Saviour, Giovanni Goritius.' Written in Hebrew on the unrolled parchment held by Isaiah is: 'Open the gates that the believers may enter' (Isaiah XXVI 2). Commissioned by the apostolic proto-notary Giovanni Goritz, it was executed between 1511–12. Vasari relates that Raphael repainted it after having seen Michelangelo's Sistine prophets. The fresco was washed by a sacristan,

according to the evidence of Celio (*Pitture . . . in Rome*, 1638) and was retouched by Daniele da Volterra. Recently Cellini restored it, removing all of the over-painting in tempera and water colour added in the 19th century, as well as some older repainting in oil (BDA, 1960). Some copies are known; one commissioned by Cardinal Federico Borromeo, in the Pinacoteca Ambrosiana in Milan; another in the gallery of the Belvedere in Vienna, attributed to Annibale Carracci; a third by Giovanni Battista Casanova in Dresden.

Preparatory sketch (detail) for 90 (Lille, Musée Wicar).

Drawing for the putto on the left in 93 (Haarlem, Teyler Museum).

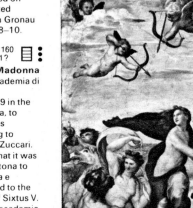

92 Pls. XXXI-XXXIII

93

Putto Rome, Accademia di San Luca

An exact copy of the putto on the left in *The Prophet Isaiah* (93). It came to its present location with the Wicar bequest (May 1834). In 1829, when it was part of the Wicar Collection, Pungileoni examined it and declared that it came from a fireplace, formerly in the Vatican, adorned with two putti holding the coat of arms of Julius II. The putti must have been detached and sold at the time of the enlargement of the Museo Vaticano. The second putto supposedly went to England. Critics have since regarded this as a work of Raphael executed immediately before or after the fresco for the Church of S. Agostino. Recently, however, Salerno (BDA, 1960) pointed out that the two putti bearing Julius II's coat of arms are still in the Vatican, having been transferred to the inside of the door (now walled up) of the Museo Clementino : they are not related to the putto in question, and present difficulties of attribution due to damage caused when they were

94

detached and to the successive layers of over-painting. The putto under discussion appears to have been executed on a concave rather than a flat surface. This would exclude its having belonged to the original composition for S. Agostino (to which Vasari seems to allude), and suggests rather the shape of a ceiling. Raphael is unlikely to have repeated a figure, using the same cartoon for a different composition. Salerno believes that this putto might be a copy which Wicar executed in 1813–14 when the Accademia di San Luca requested him to examine Raphael's fresco in S. Agostino, after which he probably helped in the restoration. Wicar initially intended to try to make a

faithful copy and only later had the idea of passing it off as the original, leaving it finally to the Accademia which issued the following receipt to Wicar's heirs : 'a putto painted in fresco on the wall, said to be by the immortal Raphael, retouched by the esteemed Cavaliere Wicar.' The remarks 'said to be' and 'retouched' reveal some uncertainty. Salerno's hypothesis is convincing and should be confirmed by a careful analysis of the work which would also clarify the technique used (Cellini, BDA, 1960).

The Stanza di Eliodoro

The second Stanza (see p. 100) takes its name from one of the wall frescoes (95 E). The decoration was begun during the second half of 1511 and completed in 1514. The last payment to Raphael was made on 1 August, 1514. The new cycle has a historical theme ; the intervention of God on the side of the Church. The outline was undoubtedly proposed by Julius II with references to his own political and religious programmes and to the vicissitudes of the papacy. On the walls are four frescoes : *The Expulsion of Heliodorus, The Mass of Bolsena, The Liberation of St Peter* and *The Repulse of Attila.* The four biblical episodes on the ceiling, depicting God's protection of the people of Israel, are related to the stories below. The wainscot is decorated with eleven caryatids in chiaroscuro (allegories of commerce, religion, law, peace, protection, nobility, navigation, abundance, pastoralism, agriculture and vine growing) and four herms with intervening tablets in simulated marble. Lower down, small panels, which look like bronze bas-reliefs, are painted with scenes portraying the prosperity of the dominions of the Church. The decorations of the base, formerly attributed to Penni or even Raphael, is today usually regarded as the work of Perino del Vaga. Cavalcaselle maintained that the caryatids were executed by Penni from a drawing by Raphael ; the remaining decoration, by other assistants. Gamba also assigned the conception of the caryatids to Raphael.

The ceiling

The ceiling is divided into four scenes, placed around a central medallion, bearing Julius II's coat of arms, and framed by diagonal bands decorated with arabesques on a gold ground. The scenes, which appear like tapestries hung between the frames and secured with *trompe l'oeil* nails and rings, represent *The Burning Bush, Jacob's Ladder,*

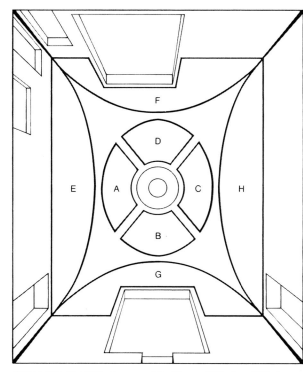

Perspective plan of the frescoes of the Stanza di Eliodoro (95); the letters refer to the Catalogue.

God Appears to Noah and *Isaac's Sacrifice.* The areas between the frames and lunettes were probably decorated by Peruzzi before Raphael began. The four Biblical episodes are described by Vasari as the work of Raphael ; Cavalcaselle and some modern critics, however, have attributed the execution to Peruzzi. A. Venturi, with the support of other critics, attributes the execution to Guglielmo di Marcillat ; Baumgart, to Penni. The poor state of preservation prevents reliable attribution.

95 ⊞ ⊗ base 390* 1511 🗐 ⦂

A. The Burning Bush
Above *The Expulsion of Heliodorus;* the episode is taken from the Bible (*Exodus*, III 2, 6 ff.). There are strong Michelangelesque and classical influences.

95 ⊞ ⊗ base 340* 1511 🗐 ⦂

B. Jacob's Ladder
Above *The Liberation of St Peter;* as God appears in a dream to Jacob, so He appears in a dream to free St Peter. The episode comes from *Genesis,* XVIII 10 ff.

95 ⊞ ⊗ base 390* 1511 🗐 ⦂

C. God Appears to Noah
Above *The Repulse of Attila;* the divine apparition saves Noah from the flood, as Rome was saved from the Huns. Taken from *Genesis* IV 8, 10 and 13, it is clearly derived from Michelangelo's ceiling of the Sistine Chapel.

95 ⊞ ⊗ base 340* 1511 🗐 ⦂

D. Isaac's Sacrifice
Abraham gave proof of unshakeable faith, but the priest of Bolsena, pictured on the wall below, doubted the

reality of transubstantiation. There is an influence from Michelangelo and classical sculpture.

The wall frescoes

95 ⊞ ⊗ base 750* 1511-12 🗐 ⦂

E. The Expulsion of Heliodorus from the Temple
In the right foreground Heliodorus, who has profaned the temple, has been thrown down and trampled by the horse of the holy messenger, while in the background the priest Onias is deep in prayer amid the shadows broken by the flickering light of the candelabra on the altar. On the left Julius II, carried by the sedan bearers, impassively watches the scene, which alludes to the inviolability of the Church's possessions and its firm intention to drive out any usurpers. More specifically, it probably refers to the defeat of the cardinals opposing the pope at the Council of Pisa, 1512. The scene takes place inside an immense temple ; the austere and compact classical temple of *The School of Athens* here becomes a succession of arcades and cupolas, punctuated by glaring lights and deep masses of shadows. The irresistible momentum of the action, in which the power of divine intervention is manifested, the violence of the movements, the extreme contrasts of chiaroscuro would have been unthinkable in the first Stanza. They indicate how Raphael's interest changed from the serene intellectual meditation of the first Stanza to the dramatic representation of historical events in this fresco. This change, both idealogical and stylistic, has been related to a renewed influence of Leonardo by Hoogewerff (C, 1925) who noted the dependence of the white horse of the holy messenger upon Leonardo's studies for the Trivulzio monument. The two chair bearers of the Pope have been traditionally identified as Marcantonio Raimondi and Giulio Romano. Vasari reproduced these two portraits

95 A

95 C

95 B

95 D

in his biographies of the two artists. Other critics believe that the second figure is Raphael himself. The severe damage to the fresco is commonly associated with the period of the 'sack' of Rome when the imperial troops quartered in the apartments apparently lit a fire in the chimney below the figure of Heliodorus. Maratta, and possibly others, carried out restorations of an inferior quality. It is sometimes argued by Cavalcaselle, for example, that this fresco was the first to be executed in the Stanza and can be dated 1511–12. Other critics, however, prefer to take *The Mass of Bolsena* first. Ortolani claims that the area on the left was added at a somewhat later date. Cavalcaselle has pointed out the work of collaborators and assigned the execution of the right portion to Giulio Romano and that of the group of women to Giovanni da Udine. The papal cortege on the left

Detail (of the figure on the left, behind the horseman) from the cartoon for 95 E (Paris, Louvre).

Studies for the figures of the women on the left in 95 E (Oxford, Ashmolean Museum).

was attributed to Raphael. However, many critics today believe that the execution of this scene, as well as the other wall frescoes, is autograph.

95 ⊞ ⊕ base 660* c. 1511 ⊟ ⦂
F. The Mass of Bolsena
The fresco extends down along the sides of the window which measures approximately 295 cm. at its widest. On the same wall Bramantino had previously painted figures of condottieri. The miracle portrayed occurred in 1263 in Bolsena. A Bohemian priest, who doubted the reality of transubstantiation, was celebrating mass at the altar of St Christine when he saw blood dripping from the consecrated Host. The festival of Corpus Christi, instituted by Urban II, originates from this incident. This choice of subject is traditionally attributed to Julius II who wished to pay homage to Sixtus IV, promoter of the cult of Corpus Christi, and also to celebrate the Church's victory in the Lateran Council which opened in May 1512. In front of the priest celebrating mass is Julius II in prayer with a group of cardinals behind him; lower down are several Swiss guards and chair bearers. Among the prelates who have been identified are Cardinal Riario with his hands crossed, and possibly Cardinal Sangiorgio with his hands together. The compositional difficulties caused by the position of the window, which is not symmetrical, have been solved by extending the platform of the altar on the right, by varying the steps and by the grouping of the figures in the foreground. The movement of the figures on the left is balanced by the immobility of the pope and his entourage. As in *The Expulsion of Heliodorus*, Raphael differentiates between the figures who participate in the action and the group of observers. In this fresco, also, the colour is very intense. The extraordinary richness of the colour has often been explained by comparison with Venetian painting. It has been suggested

95 F Pls. XL-XLIV

that Venetian artists collaborated in the decoration of the second Stanza. Wackernagel (MFK, 1909) advanced the theory that Sebastiano del Piombo painted the group of cardinals; Zampetti (*Mostra di L. Lotto,* 1953) claims that Lotto influenced the execution of the group of chair bearers; Longhi even considers Lotto the author. Gamba suggested the possibility of Hellenistic-Roman influences, derived

Possible study for the woman on the left in 95 F (Chatsworth, Duke of Devonshire).

from the numerous paintings which could be then seen in Rome, in better condition than they are today. Ortolani distinguished between the tonalism of the Venetians and Raphael's so-called 'tonalism': 'enclosed within single areas which stand out from the total composition with a freedom that the true tonalists never achieved.' Recently, Brizio (AL, 1965) re-evaluated the traditional association between Raphael and Sebastiano del Piombo, basing her arguments on chronological and stylistic considerations and on the principle that there has been too schematic an identification of the colouristic values with Venetian art and of the formal values with the school of central Italy. Colour had always been of fundamental importance in Raphael's art from his earliest years in the Marches, where links with Venice had always existed, and continuing in Urbino, where there were many Flemish paintings, and later in Florence and Rome. At the time of the Stanza di Eliodoro, Raphael was 'deeply interested in the creation of history painting, and also in achieving a more objective approach in portraiture with social and psychological overtones' (Brizio). He was scarcely likely to be attracted by the tendency to lyrical idealization, characteristic of the tradition of Giorgione. Extensive restorations of the left side of the fresco sufficiently explain a certain degeneration in style, without the necessity of having recourse to hypotheses of extensive collaboration by assistants. On the architrave is written: JVLIVS II. LIGVR. PONT. MAX. ANN. CHRIST. MDXII. PONTIFICAT. SVI. VIII.

95 ⊞ ⊕ base 660* 1513-14 ⊟ ⦂
G. The Liberation of St Peter
On the wall that Piero della Francesca had previously

frescoed, the painting extends down along the sides of the window which is the same size as the one opposite. Faithfully adhering to the account in *Acts* (XII, 6 ff.), Raphael brings together, in the style of a continuous narrative, two successive moments of the story. In the centre, above the bars of the Jerusalem prison, the angel, ablaze with light, appears to St Peter; on the right he leads the saint by the hand out of the prison past the sleeping guards, on the left, the guards are depicted at the moment of their terror-struck awakening, illuminated by the cold night light, by the glare of the torches and the flickering light on the cuirasses. The scene refers to the deliverance of Italy from the French and the preservation of the inviolability of the papacy. On a more spiritual level the deliverance of the papacy from earthly chains is implied. The subject would also have been of personal significance to Julian, for thirty-two years Cardinal of S. Pietro in Vincoli. Light is the protagonist of the story. Raphael produces new effects with extraordinary freedom and sensitiveness, portraying the miraculous event with remarkable immediacy. Two *trompe l'oeil* plaques on the architrave of the window bear the inscription: LEO.X. PONT. MAX. ANN. CHRIST. MDXIIII. PONTIFICAT. SVI II.

Cavalcaselle's conviction that this fresco was executed in 1513–14, after Julius II's death, led him to place *The Liberation* after *The Repulse;* this dating has been favourably received by some recent critics (Ragghianti, Suida, Camesasca). Others regard *The Repulse* as the later work. Traces of repainting are noticeable in the background.

95 E Pls. XXXVIII-XXXIX

95 ⊞ ⊕ base 750* ⊟ ⦂
　　　　　　　1514

H. The Repulse of Attila
On this wall Bramantino had frescoed figures of condottieri. The meeting between Pope Leo the Great and the King of the

Numerous copies can be found in the Louvre, in Sanremo, Florence, Verona, Milan, Chantilly, Loreto, Parma, Rome, New York, Fontenay-aux-Roses (Paris), etc. The original was probably painted in 1511–2.

First draft for 95 G (Florence, Uffizi). By comparison with the finished fresco, Raphael's search for a more rigid symmetry is evident.

95 G Pls. XLV-XLVII

Huns, which took place in the area of the Mincio in 452, is represented against a background of Rome. On the left can be seen a basilica, an aqueduct and the Colosseum; on the right a fire rages on Monte Mario. The Pope advances toward the hordes of Attila as SS. Peter and Paul appear in the sky armed with swords. Julius II probably intended that the story should suggest the battle of Ravenna, when the French were defeated by papal troops. After his death, however, Leo the Great was made to resemble Leo X, whose portrait already appeared in the person of the last cardinal on the left. The fresco displays the principles of asymmetrical composition which are to dominate the next Stanza. Bertini, (CDA, 1959) assigns a particularly large portion to Giulio Romano. Hartt, who fixes Giulio Romano's date of birth at 1499 rather than 1492, tends to exclude any collaboration with Raphael before 1515.

96 ⊞ ⊕ ‥‥‥‥ ⊟ °°°
　　　　　　1511-12

The Holy Family (Madonna of the Veil)
A lost work of Raphael, mentioned by Anonimo Magliabechiano, Vasari and Von Sandrart (*Der Teutschen Akademie* ... 1675), in Sta Maria del Popolo in Rome. Vögelin (*Die Madonna von Loreto*, 1870) and Cavalcaselle refused to accept Sandrart's testimony on the grounds that there is no reliable information about the painting after 1615.

97 ⊞ ⊕ 320 × 194 ⊟ ⦂
　　　　　　1511-12

Madonna of Foligno Rome, Pinacoteca Vaticana
The Madonna and Child, raised aloft, are framed by a large orange-coloured circle of light and encircled by a crown of putti; below on the left are St John the Baptist and St Francis kneeling; on the right, the donor kneeling in prayer presented to the Virgin by St Jerome. In the centre a putto holds a plaque which probably records the vow of the donor, Sigismondo de´ Conti, whose house in Foligno

Copies of 96 (Paris, Louvre; New York, Metropolitan Museum, J. Paul Getty Collection).

was struck by lightning, or a fireball, and remained undamaged. The event is illustrated in the background behind the putto. Placed in the Church of the Aracoeli, it was transferred in 1565 to the Church of Sta Anna in Foligno by the donor's niece, a nun. In 1797 it was removed to Paris by Napoleon and transferred from the original panel to canvas (1800–1). After its restitution it passed to the Pinacoteca Vaticana. The compositional unity of the two parts is achieved by the expressions and the gestures of the saints and the donor – a portrait of rare penetration. The landscape, illuminated by shafts of light and the phosphorescent flame of the fireball, has been related to the school of Ferrara and attributed to Battista Dossi by Cavalcaselle and Mendelssohn

(*Das Werk der Dossi*, 1914) and to Dosso Dossi by Longhi (*Officina ferrarese*, 1934). There is no evidence to support their hypotheses; this suggestion should be seen in relation to the larger issue of the supposed Venetian collaboration of Sebastiano del Piombo, Lotto, etc. in Raphael's work between approximately 1511 and 1514. There is no need to assume improbable collaborations if we bear in mind the fantastic and ever more complex lighting of Raphael's works of this period.

The dating is generally fixed at 1511–2; A. Venturi, nonetheless, proposes a date of around 1509. A print with some variations was made by Marcantonio Raimondi. The painting was restored in 1957–8 under the direction of Cesare Brandi.

98 ⊞ ⊕ 1511-13 ⊟ °°°

Allegories of the Months
Roma, Palazzi Vaticani
According to a document published by Müntz in June 1511, Raphael was commissioned by Julius II to complete the fresco decorations of a corridor begun by Peruzzi who, as related by Vasari, had painted 'in chiaroscuro all the months of the year and the activities concerning each month'. Raphael appears to have painted the last five of the seventeen arches of the room: one during the papacy of Julius II and four for Leo X. Although Vasari speaks of a 'corridor of the palace ... near the roof', Geymuller (quoted by Müntz) believes this could be one of the floors in the right wing of the Cortile del Belvedere, in which case the frescoes would have been destroyed when most of the building collapsed during Clement VII's papacy.

99 ⊞ ⊕ 67 × 54 ⊟ ⦂
　　　　　　1512

Portrait of a Young Woman
Florence, Uffizi
This was at one time considered a portrait of the Fornarina. It has been exhibited in the Tribuna of the Uffizi since 1589 with the designation 'Raphael.' It appeared, nevertheless, in the catalogues from 1704 to 1784 as a Giorgione. The traditional attribution to Raphael was sustained by various critics, including Quatremère de Quincy (1839), Burckhardt (1855) and Passavant; however in Missirini's translation of Quatremère de Quincy, he proposed the authorship of Sebastiano del Piombo, which found widespread agreement and was accepted by Pallucchini (*Sebastian Viniziano*, 1944) and by Salvini (*Catalogo ... degli Uffizi*, 1952 ff.) with an approximate date of 1512. There is an old copy in the Palazzo Venezia in Rome.

100 ⊞ ⊕ 107 × 80 ⊟ ⦂
　　　　　　1512

Portrait of Julius II Florence, Uffizi
Formerly owned by Vittoria della Rovere of Urbino, it passed to the Medici family.

95 H

97 Pl. XXXVII

105 Pl. LVI

100

Copy of 100 attributed to Titian (Florence, Uffizi).

99

Listed as a work of Giulio Romano on the invoice from Urbino, it was catalogued after its arrival in Florence: 'by the hand of Raphael.' It is impossible to connect this provenance with that of the portrait of Julius II executed by Raphael for the church of Sta Maria del Popolo in Rome, where it was seen by Vasari and Lomazzo (*Idea . . .*, 1590), and offered in sale by Cardinal Sfondrati to the Emperor Rudolf II (documents published by Urlichs, ZBK, 1870), since when all trace of the painting was lost. Raphael's authorship of the Uffizi picture was rejected by Passavant and the work is considered today an old copy of some merit, probably executed around 1512. Among the numerous copies, one perhaps by Titian came to Florence with the original and is now in the Pitti.

101 ▦ ✪ 132×86 1512* 目⋮

Portrait of a Cardinal Naples, Galleria Nazionale di Capodimonte
The subject has been identified as Silvio Passerini, Alessandro Farnese and Pope Paul III. The traditional attribution to Raphael was rejected by Cavalcaselle, who considers this a Florentine work of the early 16 th century. Morelli assigned it to the school of Raphael, whereas Berenson, A. Venturi and Fischel judged it to be almost entirely autograph. Its poor state of preservation makes attribution difficult.

102 ▦ ✪ 1512-13 目⋮

Portrait of Federico Gonzaga
In a letter dated 24 May, 1512, Isabella d'Este authorized Matteo Ippolito to arrange for Raphael to paint a portrait of her son Federico 'dal pecto in suso armato.' Letters sent in January and February of 1513 to the Marquis of Mantua from Gaudio and Grossino attest that Raphael had begun the work. It was probably left unfinished on the death of Julius II. On 1 January, 1512, Castiglione

Preparatory drawing for 100 (Chatsworth, Duke of Devonshire).

wrote to Federico, who had become the lord of Mantua, that the portrait had come into the possession of one of Cardinal Colonna's domestics, who would not part with it. It subsequently passed to Mantua, as related in a letter to Gonzaga from Ippolito Calandra on 28 October, 1531, in which he refers to a painting 'done by Raphael of Urbino in Rome for Your Eminence.' Subsequently it probably passed to Charles I of England and may be identified as a 'head of a beardless young man, with long hair, wearing a red hat decorated with a medallion, and a white shirt without lace. It represents the Marquis of Mantua . . . ;' described in Van der Doort's catalogue (London, 1757). According to Passavant,

it passed finally to the Lucy Collection in Charlecote Park (Warwick) in very poor condition. No further information is available.

103 ▦ ✪ diam. 65 1513-14 目⋮

Madonna and Child Between Two Angels Bearing Torches (Madonna of the Candelabra) Baltimore, Walters Art Gallery
Formerly in the Borghese Collection in Rome; traditionally attributed to Raphael. According to Cavalcaselle, supported by some modern critics, Raphael executed only the Virgin's head, leaving the rest to Giulio Romano. Dated around 1513–4; in poor condition. Two old copies were shown for several years in the National Gallery in London.

104 ▦ ✪ 88×66 1513-14 目⋮

Portrait of Giuliano De' Medici New York, Metropolitan Museum
A portrait of 'duca Giuliano' by Raphael is mentioned by Vasari. It was probably executed in 1513–4. The copy in the Metropolitan Museum in New York, which came from the Bache Collection, was regarded as a work of Raphael by Gronau, L. Venturi (*Pitture italiane in America*, 1931) and Suida; as a work of collaboration by A. Venturi and Fischel. Cavalcaselle, Gamba, Ortolani and Camesasca, on the other hand, have rightly rejected the theory of Raphael's execution of this portrait. The original has probably been lost. Beside the version in New York, there are numerous copies with variations, among which is the one in a private Swiss collection published as an original by De Maffeis (A, 1959); others are in Florence, Turin and Alnwick Castle.

105 ▦ ✪ 265×196 1513-14 目⋮

The Sistine Madonna Dresden, Gemäldegalerie
The Virgin appears between parted curtains walking solemnly on the clouds, the

Christ Child in her arms; flanking her are SS. Sixtus and Barbara. Below, in the centre foreground, two putti lean on the balustrade. Raphael's unusual choice of canvas, instead of panel, for this work has been given various explanations. According to Rumohr (*Italienische Forschungen*, III), the painting had also been envisaged as a processional standard; Vasari asserts that Raphael painted it 'for the black nuns of the Convent of San Sisto in Piacenza,' which would seem to be confirmed by the presence of the two saints particularly venerated by the convent. According to Grimme (ZBK, 1922), supported by Fischel and other recent studies, it was intended to decorate the tomb of Julius II, a theory which Alpatov (A, 1957) claims does not resolve all the enigmas of the painting. Its use as a funerary decoration would explain the half-drawn curtains in the style of funeral monuments of that period, the presence of St Barbara who brings comfort in the hour of death, and of St Sixtus, the protector of the house of Della Rovere and of the putti who were used on sarcophagi. A note by Oddone Ferrari, a nun of the Convent of S. Sisto, written toward the middle of the 18th century and quoted by Nasalli Rocca (ibid.), suggests that the painting was acquired by the nuns of Piacenza when the collection of Julius II was dispersed. According to this theory, the Madonna has the features of the famous Fornarina; St Sixtus, of Julius II; St Barbara, of Giulia Orsini, niece of the pope; and the symbolic tower and palm were added later. The portrait of Julius II in the person of St Sixtus was recognized by Cavalcaselle, Stubel (*Raffaels Sixtinische Madonna*, 1926) and Filippini (CEDA, 1925), who also maintains that St Barbara is a portrait of Lucrezia della Rovere, another niece of the pope. The most tenable of all the theories that have been advanced appears to be that of Putscher (*Raffaels Sixtinische Madonna*, 1955) who believes the *Madonna* was originally intended for the Church of S. Sisto, which was under construction at the time the painting was being executed, and that it was to serve as a blind window in the centre of the apse. There are different opinions on this point since certain historians believe that the painting was first placed on the high altar. In 1754 it was acquired by Augustus III of Saxony, who had a copy made by Nogari for its original home. After World War II, it was transferred to Moscow and then to the Gemäldegalerie. Despite all these changes of location, the painting does not appear to have sustained any serious damage (0, 1956). In *The Sistine Madonna*, Raphael's reflections on the theme of the altarpiece are resolved in one of his most original solutions. The figure of the Madonna-Mother is transformed into that of the

101

103

104

106 Pl. L

Madonna-Intercessor; the saints become mediators between the divine person and the faithful whose presence though not visible is suggested by the advancing Madonna, by the gesture of St Sixtus and by the expression of St Barbara. The Child is held by the Virgin almost like an offering, a prototype of the sacrifice for the salvation of mankind (Grimme). The Virgin appears barefooted without a halo or any adornment on her gown, but this extremely human image is redeemed by her supernatural beauty and the adoration surrounding her. The gestures and expressions – that of St Sixtus, ecstatically turned toward the Madonna, and that of St Barbara turned toward the faithful – create a chain of circular movements which enclose the Madonna and the spectator who participate together in the same action. Heaven and earth are linked with a theatrical touch by the curtains and the balustrade, on which the papal tiara is placed. By involving the spectator, the dramatic effect of the Virgin's sudden appearance is renewed. The dominant chromatic range is cold and austere, warmed by areas of yellow and red.
Critical opinion is agreed on Raphael's authorship of the work. Disagreement exists, however, as to the dating. Raphael's development of the theme of the Sacra Conversazione would place *The Sistine Madonna*, as Brizio maintains, before *St Cecilia*, which suggests a dating of around 1513–4. A conflicting opinion is held by A. Venturi, Gamba, Golzio, Ragghianti, Camesasca and Alpatov, who propose 1516.

106 ⊞ ⊗ 158×125 1513-14 🗒 ⦂
Madonna of the Linen Window (dell'Impannata)
Florence, Pitti
On the left of the Virgin and Child are St Elizabeth, in the foreground, and St Catherine; on the right, the young St John. In the background is the window covered with linen that

Plan of the architectural elements (from Fischel, 1948), of 107 and of the two groups of Prophets with angels placed above.

gives the painting its name. According to Vasari, it was executed for Bindo Altoviti; it subsequently belonged to Cosimo I de' Medici. Transferred to Paris in 1799, it was restored to Italy in 1815. The design is Raphael's but the execution is attributed almost entirely to his school. Passavant sees the hand of Raphael in the figure of the Infant Jesus; Fischel, in the head of St Elizabeth; Francini Ciaranfi (*Pitti*, 1955), in the figures of Jesus and St Elizabeth. It can be dated around 1513–4.

107 ⊞ ⊗ base 615* 1514 🗒 ⦂
Sibyls and Angels – Four Saints and Four Angels
Rome, Church of Sta Maria della Pace
The fresco encircles the arch of the first chapel on the right. In the centre a putto holds a torch, symbol of prophetic light and eternal life; on the left the Cumaean Sibyl points with her raised arm to a screed, held by an angel in flight, on which is written in Greek (as are all the inscriptions save the penultimate), 'The Resurrection of the Dead;' a putto holds a tablet with the inscription, 'There Shall Be Born;' Persica writes on a tablet supported by an angel, 'His Destiny Will Be Death;' on the right an angel indicates to the Phrygian sibyl (or Tiburtine) a tablet inscribed with, 'The Heavens Encircle the Vessel of the Earth;' followed by a putto leaning on a tombstone inscribed, 'Iam no(va) proge(nies)'; and the Tiburtine sibyl (or Cumaean), above whom is an angel with an unfurled parchment on which is written, 'I Shall Open and Resuscitate.' The identification of the sibyls, although traditional, is unlikely to be correct. The fresco was executed for Agostino Chigi, probably in 1514. Gamba is the only critic to give an earlier dating of 1512–4. The theme of the chapel is the resurrection. M. Hirst argues (JWC, 1961) that Raphael envisaged an altarpiece on this same subject. There are a number of *Resurrection* drawings which date from about this time. They show that he conceived the altarpiece in the highly dramatic language of the Eliodoro frescoes. The composition unfolds like a garland, reviving with a more complex rhythm the ideas developed in *The Virtues* of the Stanza della Segnatura (85 N). The inspiration provided by Michelangelo's

(Above) Two groups of saints and angels above in 107. (Below) The same two groups in the copy engraved by G.B.Volpato.

figures in the lunette of the Sistine Chapel is transformed with greater originality than in *Isaiah* in the Church of S. Agostino (93). The isolation of Michelangelo's figures is transformed into an unimpeded, fluent movement by Raphael. The angels are strongly reminiscent of those in the *Madonna del Baldacchino* (79). The fresco is generally regarded as by Raphael, despite the confusion due to extensive restorations. The prophets and angels in attendance and in flight (the angels in flight are at the apex of the composition) above the fresco were assigned to Raphael by Vasari in his *Lives*; yet in Vasari's biography of Viti, he attributes them to the latter artist. A. Venturi (*Grandi artisti italiani*, 1925) considers Raphael the author with the assistance of others, but not Viti whose style was too 'fifteenth-century'. It is difficult to judge because of the fresco's very poor state of preservation.

108 ⊞ ⊗ 220×136 1514 🗒 ⦂
The Ecstasy of St Cecilia
Bologna, Pinacoteca Nazionale
Her musical instruments abandoned at her feet, St Cecilia distractedly holds an organ and gazes ecstatically toward the choir of angels in the heavens. Grouped around St Cecilia are St Paul, in meditation, St John the Evangelist whose gaze meets that of St Augustine on the right, and Mary Magdalene looking at the spectator. Vasari relates that Lorenzo Pucci, 'Cardinal of the Four Saints', commissioned this work for the Church of S. Giovanni in Monte in Bologna. Vasari, however, has confused Lorenzo Pucci, who

commissioned the chapel of St Cecilia in the Church of S. Giovanni in Monte, with Antonio Pucci, bishop of Bologna at the time the painting was executed, and elected cardinal only in 1531. Filippini (CEDA, 1925) published a document of the Convent of S. Giovanni, which records that Elena, wife of Benedetto dall'Oglio, commissioned the altarpiece in 1514. Removed to Paris by Napoleon in 1798, it was transferred from panel to canvas in 1801. Chastel noted that the choice of the four saints was not accidental; they evoke 'affective mysticism' and the 'power of ecstasy.' In this picture, Raphael makes ecstasy itself the sole theme of the painting. This revolutionary approach is described by Brizio (AL, 1965): 'With a single stroke, Raphael transposes the sacred image to the emotions, allowing the divinity to reveal itself from within the soul of St Cecilia. This treatment of the theme corresponds with the more formal rendering of expressions and gestures and the extreme balance and symmetry of composition, which made the St Cecilia unpopular with critics of the Romantic period after centuries of esteem. The dating is almost unanimously given as 1514. Longhi (*Officina ferrarese*, 1934) noted that the St Cecilia

Study for the figure of the Persian (?) sibyl in 107 (Oxford, Ashmolean Museum).

Copy after a lost drawing for the angel, left, and the arm of a sibyl in 107 (as above).

108 Pls. XLVIII-IL

slightly influenced Emilian painting of the next decade. Vasari asserts that the still life of musical instruments was by Giovanni da Udine. Other critics see the hand of various students of Raphael. There are signs of repainting and some of the colours have changed in value. There are several copies.

109 ⊞ ⊘ diam. 71 1514 ⊟:
Madonna and Child With the Infant St John (Madonna of the Chair) Florence, Pitti
Part of the Medici Collection until the first half of the 16th century, it then passed from the Uffizi to the Pitti at the beginning of the 18th century. It was transferred by Napoleon to Paris where it remained from 1799–1815. There is disagreement about the dating, which can probably be set at 1514.

110 ⊞ ⊘ 68×55 1514 ⊟:
Madonna and Child With the Infant St John (Madonna of the Curtain) Munich, Alte Pinakothek
According to Conca (*Descrizione... della Spagna*, 1793) this picture formed part of the Escorial Collection. At the beginning of the 19th century it passed to England, where it was acquired by Prince Ludwig of Bavaria. Cavalcaselle rejects the traditional attribution to Raphael, and credits Domenico Alfani with the execution from drawings by Raphael. Later critics accepted Raphael's authorship. Cavalcaselle, supported by Morelli and others, regards this as a variation of the *Madonna of the Chair* (109),

109 Pl. LII

110

111

whereas Ortolani believes it 'preceded and prepared the ground for the *Madonna of the Chair*.' The dating fluctuates between 1514 and 1516.

111 ⊞ ⊘ 215×158 1514* ⊟:
Madonna of the Fish Madrid, Prado
Holding the fish in his right hand, Tobias is presented to the Virgin by the angel Raphael; on the other side kneels St Jerome with the lion. In a letter dated 20 March, 1524, Summonte relates that he had seen the painting in the Church of S. Domenico in Naples, where it remained until 1638, when it passed to the Spanish viceroy, the Duke of Medina; taken to Spain in 1644, it belonged to Philip IV who left it to the Escorial. From 1813–22 it was

112

kept in France, where it had been brought by Napoleon; during this time it was transferred from panel to canvas. Critics agree on the collaboration of assistants; the date has been set as late as 1517 by Berenson, De Sotomayor, etc., but is currently set between 1512–4. Various copies are known in Naples, the Escorial, Valladolid, etc.

112 ⊞ ⊘ 90×60 1514* ⊟:
Portrait of Cardinal Fedra Inghirami Boston, Isabella Stewart Gardner Museum
This painting remained in the Inghirami house in Volterra until the beginning of the 20th century when it passed to the Gardner Museum. Cavalcaselle considered it a copy of the one in the Pitti (113) and not the original. Those who believed it to be the original are Morelli, Durand-Gréville (AS, 1907), Gamba and Suida. Gronau regards both as autograph works, as do Marangoni (*La Galleria Pitti*, 1951), Carli, Francini Ciaranfi (*Pitti*, 1955), Camesasca and Monti. Fischel, on the other hand, regards both as copies and the original as lost. The dating fluctuates 1512–4.

113 ⊞ ⊘ 90×62 1515-16 ⊟:
Portrait of Cardinal Fedra Inghirami Florence, Pitti
Formerly in the collection of Cardinal Leopoldo de' Medici; it was removed to Paris by Napoleon in 1799 and restored to the Pitti in 1815. Judged autograph by Passavant, A. Venturi and Pittaluga, who did not mention the Boston version (112). Gamba regards it as a

copy executed by Daniele da Volterra. Durand-Gréville first assigned only the execution of the face to Raphael (AS, 1907) and later recognized the whole work as by Raphael (ibid., 1910), dating it later than the Boston portrait (see 112 for other opinions). In accordance with Durand-Gréville's hypothesis, the portrait can be dated around 1515-6.

114 ⊞ ⊘ 82×67 1514-15 ⊟:
Portrait of Baldassar Castiglione Paris, Louvre
This work is mentioned in a letter from Bembo to Castiglione on 19 April, 1516. Castiglione himself brought it to Mantua where it remained until 1609. It then passed to Holland to the collection of the merchant Luca van Uffelem; subsequently, to

113 Pl. LIII

Madrid and Paris, to the collection of Cardinal Mazarin, from whom it passed to the King of France. Undoubtedly painted before 1516, it is almost unanimously dated around 1514–5. There are numerous copies, one of which is a water colour by Rembrandt and

Copy of 114, painted, possibly in 1629 in Madrid, by Peter Paul Rubens (London, Seilern Collection).

114 Pl. LIV

III

inspired his engraving of a self-portrait of 1640, and another by Rubens who probably saw the original in Madrid. This is a portrait of the author of *Il Cortegiano*, Castiglione, a friend who represented for Raphael 'the ultimate in perfection of the culture of Urbino, Florence and Rome.' Castiglione is presented through his 'idea;' the portrait becomes the expression of the ideal of aesthetic and spiritual perfection, defined in *Il Cortegiano*, which, as Chastel observes, is but 'the neoplatonic ideal, without the theology of Ficino.' There is a harmonious marriage of sensitivity and sureness, self-possession, elegance and courtesy. In good condition, despite the over-cleaning of the original varnish and retouching of the beard.

115 A

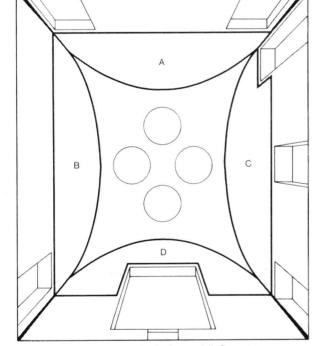

Plan in perspective (see plan for the Stanza della Segnatura on page 100) relating to the frescoes of the Stanza dell'Incendio di Borgo (115); the letters refer to the Catalogue.

Stanza of the Fire in the Borgo

Formerly called the stanza 'of the Borgia tower' (see page 100), it took its present name from one of the wall frescoes (115 A). This is the first Stanza of Julius II's apartments and was frescoed from 1514 to July 1517 after the Stanza della Segnatura and the Stanza di Eliodoro. The themes of these frescoes are historical and political; they are divided into four episodes in which the leading figures are Leonine popes (in honour of Leo X). A letter to Raphael from Castiglione in 1514 suggests that the episodes were chosen by the latter. The four tondos of the ceiling, with sacred scenes painted by Perugino in 1507–8, were preserved by Raphael out of affection for his teacher, as Vasari claims, rather than because of the speed of the execution, as Cavalcaselle believed, or because of lack of assistants in his workshop. The figures in yellow monochrome of Charlemagne, Astolfo, Godefroy de Bouillon, Lothario I and Ferdinand the Catholic, and the caryatids in chiaroscuro which decorate the wainscot, were executed by Giulio Romano. The extensive collaboration of Raphael's assistants in the decoration of the Stanza, which occurred in most of Raphael's under-takings of the last years, is seen in a definite decline in the execution of certain of the frescoes. This has led many critics to speak of an early decline of Raphael's creative ability (though barely thirty years old). The artist, according to this view, had become involved in a sterile confrontation with Michelangelo and transformed into a contractor of works which he had to leave almost completely to his young assistants. Raphael's work during this period shows not a rapid degeneration, but rather an uninterrupted flow of ideas and new solutions. As his commitments widened in an amazing burst of creativity, the opportunities for participating in the execution of his works became increasingly limited. It has been proved that much of the execution of Raphael's ideas was partially, and in some cases completely, handed over his bottega, but this does not justify a negative view of Raphael's later activity. Indeed, most of the design of these frescoes can be attributed to Raphael, and this despite the fact that from 1514 he undertook a wide range of commissions including frescoes, altarpieces, the cartoons for the tapestries intended for the Sistine Chapel, architectural work (having succeeded Bramante as architect of St Peter's) and the studies of Roman antiquities, which led him to the idea of drawing up a plan of ancient Rome.

115 ⊞ ⊕ base 670* 1514 ⊟ ⦂
A. The Fire in the Borgo
This fresco illustrates an episode from the year 847 taken from the *Liber pontificalis*. As Leo IV gives the blessing, he extinguishes a fire raging in the Borgo, a section of Rome. The figures and the architecture clearly refer to Virgil's account of the burning of Troy, so that the miracle appears in a context of heroic classicism. Aeneas, carrying his father, Anchises, with his son Ascanius at his side is recognizable on the left. The Corinthian colonnade is taken from the Temple of Mars Ultor, the building in the right foreground recalls the Temple of Saturn. The background, where the pope can be seen, has a Bramantesque quality in the rusticated base and the loggia with the motif of the windows later called 'Serlian'. Further back is the old façade of St Peter's with its mosaics. The references, both classical and modern, contained in the fresco correspond to the ideals of a 'latinized' culture, promoted by the literati of Leo X's court. The composition is much more scenographic than that of preceding works. The void in the centre and the character of the architecture draw attention to the distant figure of the pope; this idea was very popular in the 17th century. This theatrical approach could be an indication of Raphael's new interests in stage designs, as related in a letter from an envoy of the Estes to the Duke of Ferrara on 2 March, 1519, referring to Raphael's stage sets for a performance of Ariosto's *Gli Suppositi*. The fresco has been aptly described by Ortolani as 'a laboratory for a new language'; it uses an idiom that was to spread not only in Italy but throughout Europe, based on classical prototypes. A definition of this idiom as 'eclectic' would overlook its historical importance, mistaking as purely passive what has rightly been defined as 'an experimental method for the expressive capacity of the historical language of art', and would not take into account the fundamental character of Raphael's imagination. Some critics believe that the execution of the fresco was left mainly to Raphael's assistants; according to Cavalcaselle, the left side and part of the right can be assigned to Giulio Romano; the group of women in the centre, to Giovanni da Udine. The sections attributed to Raphael by Gamba, are the head of the young girl, turning as she receives the two vases, several figures in the background and scattered details. Other critics, like Oberhuber (JKS, 1962) maintain that most of the fresco is autograph. The date of the fresco may be as late as 1514. A. Venturi prefers the date 1515. Extensive repainting is evident.

115 B

115 ⊞ ⊕ base 770* 1514-15 ⊟ ⦂
B. The Battle of Ostia
This work, which alludes to Leo X's unsuccessful attempt to launch a crusade against the Turks, illustrates an episode from the *Liber pontificalis* in which the pontifical galleys are attacked in the waters of Ostia by the Arab fleet which is then dispersed by a storm (849). On the left the figure of Leo IV giving thanks is a portrait of Leo X. Recognizable among his retinue are cardinals Bibbiena and Giulio de' Medici; in the centre where the two fleets are engaged in battle stands the tower of Ostia. In the right foreground are some Moslem prisoners; these figures have been attributed to Giulio Romano; the architecture and ships, to Giovanni da Udine; Leo X and the cardinals are possibly the work of Raphael. A large part of the extensive repainting was done by Maratta. The execution can be dated 1514-5.

Study of the two figures on the left of 115 B (Vienna, Albertina).

112

115 ⊞ ✦ base 770* 1516-17 ▤ ⁞

C. The Coronation of Charlemagne

This portrayal of Charlemagne's coronation in the basilica of St Peter's probably alludes to the concordat made in Bologna in 1515 between Leo X and François I of France, who are represented respectively by Pope Leo III and Charlemagne. Vasari identifies the young man kneeling beside the emperor as Ippolito de' Medici; the architecture may refer to the progress of the construction of the new St Peter's. There are a number of drawings by Raphael for the fresco, but the inferior quality of the execution suggests that it was left entirely to assistants (Penni, Raffaellino del Colle and perhaps Giulio Romano). Cavalcaselle and Gamba have assigned several portraits in the group of bishops on the right to Raphael. The fresco was probably completed before May 1517 and precedes the *Oath of Leo III* which bears the date of the completion of the Stanza.

115 C

115 ⊞ ✦ base 670* 1517 ▤ ⁞

D. The Oath of Leo III

This painting, which extends down along the sides of the window, illustrates an episode from the *Liber pontificalis*: Leo III, in the presence of Charlemagne and the clergy in St Peter's, takes the oath denying the accusations of Adrian I's nephews, while from above come the words (written on a screed below the fresco) *Dei non hominum est episcopos iudicare* (23 December, 800). The allusion is to the Lateran Council's confirmation in 1516 of the papal bull of Boniface the III, *Unam sanctam*, sanctioning the principle of papal responsibility to God alone. The execution, which is of very poor quality, is traditionally attributed to Penni and Giovanni da Udine; Hartt assigns it to Raffaellino del Colle. Two *trompe l'oeil* tablets on the architrave bear the inscription: LEO. X. PONT. MAX. ANNO. CHRISTI. MCCCCCXVII. PONTIFICAT SVI. ANNO IIII.

115 D

The tapestry cartoons

The series of cartoons for the tapestries for the Sistine Chapel (discussed below in 116 A-G) are in the collection of H.M. the Queen and on loan to the Victoria and Albert Museum in London. Raphael received the commission from Leo X late in 1514. On 15 June, 1515, Raphael received three hundred ducats in partial payment for the cartoons or drawings to be sent to Flanders to be made into tapestries. Another 134 ducats were remitted on 20 December, 1516, perhaps as the final payment. In July 1517 the first tapestry had been completed and was seen by Cardinal Luis d'Aragon in Brussels in the shop of the tapestry-maker, Pieter van Aelst. A report from the Venetian ambassador to the Vatican reveals that by July 1519 three tapestries had arrived in Rome, followed by four others by the end of the year. All seven were displayed on St Stephen's Day in the Sistine Chapel, as related in De Grassis' *Diarium* and in a note by Michiel on 20 December. According to the note, the cartoons included *The Miraculous Draught of Fishes*, *The Charge to St Peter*, *The Martyrdom of St Stephen*, *The Conversion of Saul*, *The Healing of the Lame Man*, *The Blinding of Elymas* and *The Sacrifice of Lystra*. The remaining three (*The Preaching of St Paul*, *St Paul in Prison* and *The Death of Ananias*) probably arrived shortly afterwards. The cartoons, which were cut into pieces for the weaving process, remained in Brussels with the tapestry-maker who made several other series from them and, as was the custom, probably lent them to other shops. In some of the series which were woven later (Berlin, Vienna, Madrid, Mantua) *St Paul in Prison* is missing. There is no information about the corresponding cartoon, nor for that of *The Martyrdom of St Stephen*. The cartoon of *The Conversion of Saul* is also lost, and there is no further information about it after 1528. The other seven cartoons were purchased in Genoa in 1623 by Sir Francis Crane, director of the Mortlake factory, on behalf of the Prince of Wales, the future Charles I, on the advice – so tradition has it – of Rubens. When the collection of Charles I was sold, the cartoons were taken over by Cromwell who preserved them in boxes in the Banqueting House in Whitehall. After the Restoration they were returned to the Crown; an attempt by Charles II to sell them to the Gobelins Factory was thwarted by the government. At the end of the 17th century they were placed in a specially built gallery in Hampton Court by order of William III, who had them reassembled and glued to canvas and restored by William Cook. In 1713 they were moved to Buckingham Palace and after several other changes of location, they were lent to the Victoria and Albert Museum in 1865.

In executing the cartoons, Raphael bore in mind the fact that in weaving the design would be reversed. Many of the compositions are not symmetrical but develop dramatically from right to left in the cartoons and in the opposite direction in the tapestries. This latter is the normal direction our eyes travel when reading. Raphael, bearing in mind the weaver's restricted range of colours, used tempera in soft tonalities with large masses of light and shade. Despite Van Orley's supervision of the weavers, they partially altered the compositions by hardening the features of the figures and the elements of landscape and by introducing gold and decorative elements. In Vasari's life of Raphael, he states that 'Raphael drew and coloured in his hand all the cartoons in the exact form and size needed;' in his biography of Penni, he mentions the collaboration of the 'young men,' that is, the workshop. Passavant and Cavalcaselle assigned the cartoons to Raphael with the collaboration of Giulio Romano and Penni; whereas Dollmayr (JKS, 1895) maintained that all seven remaining cartoons were the exclusive work of Penni. This theory had some popularity, but has been almost unanimously rejected in recent critical studies, in which the prevalent tendency is to attribute most of the work to Raphael. The series, in fact, presents a strongly unitary character.

'A new sense of monumentality is created which, unlike the tormented plasticity of Michelangelo, establishes a harmony in the movement of the emotions within a balanced composition' (Bertini, CDA, 1961).

J. White and J. Shearman (AB, 1958) have convincingly argued an order for the tapestries in the Sistine Chapel which reverses the order given in the older literature. According to their theory, which takes into account the function of light in the Renaissance, the Peter stories were to hang on the North wall, the Paul stories on the South. The sequences began at the altar, with *The Stoning of St Stephen* on the left side, *The Miraculous Draught of Fishes* on the right. The tapestries are fitted out with partially removable borders which are related to their location in the Sistine Chapel. The lateral borders are decorated with different motifs of grotesques, the others serve as a wainscot, illustrating in

Study for a standing youth (Paris, Louvre) for Christ in 116 B.

grisaille episodes from the life of Leo X or St Paul.

116 ⊞ ✦ 360×400 1515 ▤ ⁞

A. The Miraculous Draught of Fishes

This episode, also referred to as *The Conversion of St Peter*, is taken from a passage in *St Luke* (V 4ff.). Raphael's authorship is practically undisputed. The story is set against a background of a vast and luminous landscape, as in *The Charge to St Peter* in which Christ also appears.

116 ⊞ ✦ 345×535 1515 ▤ ⁞

B. The Charge to St Peter

Also referred to as *Pasce oves meas* ('feed my sheep'), this episode comes from the well-known passage of the *Gospel according to St John* (XXI 15ff). Brizio noted that the figure of Christ, as in *The Miraculous Draught*, is the least

116 A

116 B

116 C

116 D

Tapestry derived from 116 C (Roma, Pinacoteca Vaticana).

monumental and dramatic; he is isolated and set off through effects of luminosity and a barely perceptible distance separating Him from the others.

116 ⊞ ⊗ 385×445 1515 ⊟⦂

C. The Blinding of Elymas
Inspired by an episode from *Acts* (XIII 8ff). Under the pre-consul's chair is written: L. SERGIVS PAVLLVS/ASIAE PROCOS / CHRISTIANAM FIDEM / AMPLECTITVR / SAVLI PREDICATIONE; it reads from left to right even in the cartoon. In poor condition.

116 E

116 F

116 G

116 ⊞ ⊗ 350×540 1515 ⊟⦂
D. The Sacrifice of Lystra
Having cured a lame man in the city of Lystra, St Paul is mistaken for Mercury; he manages to escape the crowd who wish to offer him a sacrifice in accordance with pagan ritual (*Acts*, XIV 7 ff.).

116 ⊞ ⊗ 390×520 1515 ⊟⦂
E. The Healing of the Lame Man
St Peter, accompanied by John, heals a lame man at the gate called Beautiful in the Temple of Solomon in Jerusalem (*Acts*, III lff.). The twisted columns reproduce the ones in old St Peter's which were supposed to have come from the Temple of Solomon.

116 ⊞ ⊗ 390×440 1515 ⊟⦂
F. The Preaching of St Paul
St Paul preaches from the Areopagus of Athens (*Acts*, XVII 17 ff.).

116 ⊞ ⊗ 385×440 1515 ⊟⦂
G. The Death of Ananias
This episode comes from a passage of *Acts* (V lff.) concerning St Peter's punishment of a Christian who evaded his duty to deliver his possessions to the community. The symmetry of the composition and its intensely scenographic quality were much admired by Goethe and Grim. The cartoon is mostly autograph.

116 ⊞ ⊗ 1515 ⊟⦂
H. The Martyrdom of St Stephen
The cartoon was lost in the 16th century. The episode comes from *Acts* (VII, 55–59).

117

116 ⊞ ⊗ 1515 ⊟⦂
I. The Conversion of Saul
This episode is taken from *Acts* (IX 3ff). The cartoon belonged to Cardinal Grimani in Venice and was seen by Michiel in 1521 and in 1528. It was subsequently lost.

116 ⊞ ⊗ 1515 ⊟⦂
J. St Paul in Prison
Also called *The Earthquake*, referring to the cataclysm which occurred while St Paul was in prison (*Acts* XVI 24ff.), represented here by the gigantic figure shaking the foundations of the building. The cartoon was lost in the late 16th century.

117 ⊞ ⊗ 209×107 1515? ⊟⦂
St Peter Rome, Pinacoteca Vaticana
Fra Bartolommeo was commissioned in 1514 to paint this work and a companion piece portraying St Paul for the Church of S. Silvestro al Quirinale in Rome. According to Vasari, it was subsequently entrusted to Raphael for completion. Numerous critics

accepted Vasari's information, including Berenson, Ortolani and Redig de Campos. A. Venturi favours the theory that it was completed by one of Raphael's assistants, but Ragghianti and Camesasca rejected the attribution.

118 ⊞ ⊗ 61×45 1515* ⊟⦂
Portrait of Bindo Altoviti(?)
Washington D.C., National Gallery of Art
This work passed from the Altoviti Palace in Rome to the one in Florence; acquired by Ludwig I of Bavaria, it remained in the Munich gallery until 1936 when it was brought by Samuel H. Kress; it subsequently passed to its present location. Vasari mentions that Raphael 'painted for Bindo Altoviti his portrait when he was a young man.' This information was variously interpreted. Some critics (Ruhmor, Mariette, Grim) believe that Raphael painted a self-portrait which he gave to Altoviti; others (Lanzi, Wicar, Passavant, Müntz, Springer, Cavalcaselle, etc.), followed by more recent art-historians, maintain that the subject was Altoviti himself. The dating fluctuates between 1512–5. An alternative theory holds that Giulio Romano carried out much of the execution. Hartt has

118

119

attributed the entire work to Romano, dating it 1520–4.

119 ⊞ ⊗ 59×44 1515? ⊟⦂
Portrait of a Young Man
Paris, Louvre
Formerly considered a self-portrait by Raphael. The theory of Raphael's authorship, with the approximate date of 1515, persisted (even after the work was no longer considered a self-portrait) until rejected by Morelli (1892), who favoured Bachiacca, and by A. Venturi,

who proposed Rondani. Berenson first assigned it to Sogliani and then reverted doubtfully to the original attribution; Gamba (BDA, 1924–5), supported by most contemporary critics, proposed Parmigianino.

120 ⊞ ⊗ 120×92 1515 ⊟⦂
Portrait of a Young Man
Budapest, Szépmüvészeti Museum
Formerly assigned to Raphael in the Este Collection in Modena; it passed to its present location in 1895 from the Scarpa Collection in Motta di Livenza. The original attribution was taken up by Garas (AHAH,

120

1953), but recent critics have almost unanimously assigned it to Sebastiano del Piombo, following Cavalcaselle; Pallucchini (*Sebastian Viniziano*, 1944) dates it around 1515.

121 ⊞ ⊗ 65×64 1516 ⊟⦂
Portrait of a Woman (The Lady with a Veil) Florence, Pitti
Mentioned by Vasari, Borghini (*Il Riposo*, 1584) and Bocchi (*Bellezze di Firenze*, 1591) in Florence in the house of the merchant Matteo Botti; it passed to the Medici in 1619. Passavant noted the resemblance to the Virgin in *The Sistine Madonna* (105). Morelli advanced the hypothesis that the subject was the Fornarina which was accepted by Cavalcaselle, Gruyer and Ridolfi (ASSA, 1891). Different opinions were put forward by Springer, who attributed it to Raphael, and by Filippini, who identified the subject as Lucrezia della Rovere (CEDA, 1925). Raphael's authorship, rejected

121 Pl. LV

Tapestries derived from 116 H, I and J (Roma, Pinacoteca Vaticana).

by Cavalcaselle, Burckhardt, Müntz and Bode, was upheld by Ridolfi and most modern critics. Dated around 1516; there are traces of repainting.

122 ⊞⊘ 86×65 1516*
Portrait of Cardinal Bibbiena Florence, Pitti
This work passed to the Medici from the Della Rovere Collection and was listed in the inventory as a work of Raphael. From 1799–1815 it was in Paris, where it had been taken by Napoleon. Passavant and Jahn Rusconi (*R. Galleria Pitti*, 1937) considered it a copy of the Cardinal in the Prado (88). It is generally regarded as by the School of Raphael or as an old copy of a lost autograph work. A strip of canvas was added to the bottom with part of the arm and fingers of the left hand. In a poor state of preservation.

123 ⊞⊘ 76×107 1516
Portrait of Andrea Navagero and Agostino Beazzano (?) Rome, Galleria Doria Pamphilj
The identification of the two subjects is not certain, but it is accepted almost unanimously. A painting of these two Venetian writers, on wood, not canvas, is recorded by Michiel in the house of Bembo in Padua. Bembo wrote to Bibbiena that Raphael painted a portrait of the two men while they were staying in Rome in 1516. In 1538, nine years after Navagero's death, Beazzano acquired the painting from his friend Bembo. According to Passavant and Cavalcaselle, the canvas here listed is not identifiable with the painting mentioned by Michiel, but is instead a Venetian copy; this opinion was received favourably by most modern critics. Morelli and Gamba believe that this is entirely autograph. A. Venturi suggested that this is an unfinished work by Raphael.

124 ⊞⊘ 1516
Mosaics of the Chigi Chapel
The mosaic of the dome of the Chigi Chapel in Sta Maria del Popolo in Rome marked the end of the construction of the chapel, which was designed entirely by Raphael. It was the first time that a project had been entirely under the control of one man: sculpture, painting and architecture were conceived as a unity. In this respect the chapel prefigures the Baroque. Raphael prepared the cartoons for the mosaics which were

122

executed by Luigi de Pace of Venezia. The cartoons are no longer in existence, but there are some of Raphael's preparatory studies at Oxford and at Lille, which Bertini (CA, 1961) rightly regards as 'among his most significant drawings.' The dome is divided into eight sections illustrated with pagan deities, cut off below the waist, symbolizing the planets; enclosed within archways representing the vault of heaven, the figures are surmounted by angels who, according to neoplatonic philosophy, limit the powers of the stars directing their course (Chastel). In the centre of the dome, surrounded by angels, is God the Father

124

123

dramatically foreshortened, his arms raised in a gesture of reception. The decoration, which recalls early Christian and pagan motifs, is original and has been closely related to the architecture. Since the existing altarpiece, a *Nativity*, contradicts the apparent theme of the chapel, which is a 'Triumph over Death', it is probable that Raphael may have intended an *Assumption of the Virgin*, more in keeping with the general theme. J. Shearman, who proposed this theory (JWC, 1961) has related a number of drawings (Oxford, Stockholm) to this.

125 ⊞⊘ 1516
The Stufetta of Cardinal Bibbiena Rome, Palazzo Vaticano
The *stufetta* or bathroom (a square room measuring 2.52 metres on each side, with a cross-vaulted ceiling) was part of Cardinal Bibbiena's apartments in the Vatican, next to the third-floor loggias. The fresco and stucco decorations, which are similar to those of the *Domus Aurea*, were executed in the first half of 1516, as recorded in two letters from Bembo to Bibbiena: the first on 19 April, 1516, asking for new mythological motifs to illustrate; the second on 20 June of the same year announcing the completion of the works. In the centre of the east and west walls are placed respectively a door and a window; each of the other two walls has a central niche surmounted by a slab of marble with a mask. Slender grotesques ornament the ceiling and the lunette; on each side of the door, the window and the

Study for the centre mosaic (God the Father and Angels) for 124 (Oxford, Ashmolean Museum).

Copy after a study for the mosaic depicting the planet Mars for 124 (Lille, Musée Wicar).

Study for 124 depicting an angel and the planet Jove for (Oxford, Ashmolean Museum).

niches are panels (66 cm. by about 30 cm.) frescoed with mythological scenes: *Venus and Adonis* and a destroyed panel on the north wall; *The Birth of Erichthonius* and *The Birth of Venus* on the east wall; *Venus and Cupid Led by Dolphins* and *Venus Wounded by Cupid* on the south wall; *Pan and Syrinx* and a destroyed panel (probably portraying Venus pulling out a thorn, as she appears in Dente's engraving) on the west wall. Under each of the eight scenes are smaller panels with putti, against a black ground, on carts drawn by tortoises, snails, dragons and butterflies. The *stufetta* was described by Pelleton (*Cabinet de l'amateur*, 1844) as Julius II's bathroom and was known in the 19th century as Julius II's retiring room. It was later turned into a chapel by Camuccini who had the walls covered with boards and the ceiling with canvas. When it was restored, Dollmayr (ASA, 1890) identified the source of the mythological episodes, suggested by Bibbiena, as Ovid and Servus; a study was also made by Hoffmann (*Raffael als Architekt*, 1911). Passavant and Cavalcaselle attributed the major part of the execution to Raphael; Dollmayr assigned to Giulio Romano the ornamental motifs and the execution, from designs by Raphael, of all the panels with the exception of *The Birth of Erichthonius*, which he assigned to Penni. This opinion was for the most part upheld by De Vito Battaglia (A, 1926), who attributed the last panel to a modest assistant. Hartt (*Giulio Romano*, 1958) assigns to Giulio Romano the scenes of *Venus and Adonis* and *Pan and Syrinx*, but he also rightly points out the importance of Raphael's invention and, in harmony with Raphael's ever increasing archeological interests, his astonishing capacity for recreating antiquity more classically than the Roman models he had at hand.

126 ⊞⊘ 1516
The Elephant Annone
Formerly in Rome, The Vatican Wall
When the elephant Annone, a gift to Leo X from King Manuel of Portugal, died, Raphael was engaged to paint this animal, which had had great popularity

in Rome, on one of the gates of the Vatican wall. The epitaph that accompanied the fresco was lost, but appeared in a copy executed after 1538 by Francisco de Hollanda in a note book now in the Escorial. The date MDXVI. 8.IUNI can be deciphered.

127 ⊞⊘ 72×56 1516-17
Portrait of a Young Man Cracow, Czartoryski Museum
This work was copied by Van Dyck, probably in Italy, in the sketchbook now in the British Museum; it was acquired by Prince Adam Czartoryski in 1807. According to Gamba, the left side of the painting was cut

Putto on a cart drawn by a snail; one of the scenes against a black ground for 125.

Venus and Cupid Led by Dolphins; part of the cycle for 125 (south wall).

Venus and Adonis; part of the cycle for 125 (north wall)

Venus Wounded by Cupid; part of the cycle for 125 (south wall).

115

127

128

off, and it was cleaned too vigorously. The collaboration of assistants, particularly Giulio Romano, was noted by A. Venturi. The date fluctuates from 1512–4 to 1518–9 (Gamba and A. Venturi). An intermediary date of 1516–7 would seem more likely.

128 🔲⊕ 135×142 1516–17 📋⋮
The Young St John Paris, Louvre
Executed for Cardinal Gouffier de Boissy, whose coat of arms appears next to that of La Trémouille; it subsequently passed to other French collections. Traditionally attributed to Raphael; Cavalcaselle assigned it to his bottega. Morelli assigned it to Sebastiano del Piombo, but Pallucchini (*Sebastian Viniziano*, 1944) rejected this theory; Frizzoni (A, 1906) supported Raphael's authorship, followed by most recent critics, although the collaboration of assistants is evident in the execution. In a poor state of preservation.

129 🔲⊕ 74×63 1517 📋⋮
Portrait of a Violinist Paris, E. de Rothschild Collection
Dated M.D.X.VIII; Benkard, however, claimed that the last three Roman numerals were added at a later date. Formerly in the Sciarra Collection in Rome. The attribution to Raphael, supported by Passavant, Cavalcaselle and Müntz, etc., was rejected by Morelli in favour of Sebastiano del Piombo, an opinion shared by later critics, with the exception of Propping (*Die künstlerische Laufbahn des Sebastiano del Piombo*, 1892).

130 🔲⊕ 1517 📋⋮
The Loggia di Psiche Rome, Villa Farnesina
The gallery on the ground floor of the Farnesina, which originally opened onto the garden, was decorated for Agostino Chigi with the story

of Psyche taken from Apuleus' *The Golden Ass*. The loggia is transformed into a luminous pergola festooned with fruit and flowers that divide the ceiling into sections between which the figures stand out against the azure blue of the sky. The story unfolds in the ten spandrels (measuring 4.05 metres at the widest point), four on each side of the longer walls and one at each end of the room, with the two final episodes on the ceiling, depicting *The Council of the Gods* and *The Marriage Feast of Cupid and Psyche*, which are painted like tapestries framed with flowering borders. Between the spandrels fourteen compartments (base 3.38 metres) are decorated with cupids accompanied by animals and the attributes of various gods. The spandrels are frescoed with representations of *Venus and Cupid; Cupid and the Graces; Venus with Ceres and Juno; Venus Ascending Mount Olympus; Venus and Jove; Mercury; Psyche being Transported by Cupids; Venus*

Study for Venus and Psyche *for the fresco 130 by Giulio Romano (?) (Paris, Louvre).*

Study (figures above, on the right) for The Marriage, *130 by Giulio Romano (?) (Windsor, Royal Library).*

Engraving by M. A. Raimondi of The Apostle John; *related to 131.*

and Psyche; Cupid and Jove; Mercury and Psyche. The conception is Raphael's, since he made a number of drawings for the single scenes, but the execution was left entirely to the bottega; Penni, Raeffaellino del Colle, Giulio Romano and other minor assistants. The splendid festoons were painted by Giovanni da Udine. J. Shearman has analyzed the literary sources of the frescoes

129

and suggested a reconstruction of the lost scenes (JKS, 1964). The cycle, dated 1518 by Berenson and 1518–9 by Suida and Hartt, was undoubtedly completed by the end of 1517. In a letter of 1 January, 1518 Leonardo Sellaio, having seen the frescoes, announced to Michelangelo 'a despicable thing for a great master; far worse than the last Stanza of the palace.' Extensive damage obliged Maratta to reinforce the plaster, strengthening the ceiling with 850 copper studs. Maratta repainted the background of the sky and the outlines of the figures. Part of the repainting was removed during the 1930 restorations directed by Sartorio.

131 🔲⊕ 1517 📋○
The Apostles Rome, Palazzo Vaticano
Vasari records in his biography of Giovanni da Udine that 'in another room . . . where the *cubicolari* (grooms) are, Raphael of Urbino painted certain tabernacles with some very beautiful, life-size apostles in chiaroscuro . . . but this work was shortlived; when Paul IV had his little rooms and closets built, he tore down the room and deprived the Vatican of a singular work.' In his biography of Taddeo Zuccari, Vasari also relates that the Apostles, which Raphael executed in clay, were knocked down by Paul IV and were redone by Taddeo and Federigo Zuccari. The engravings which were made after Raphael's originals by Raimondi reveal a stylistic similarity with the tapestry cartoons; this would suggest that the frescoes were executed around 1517.

132 🔲⊕ 306×230 1517 📋⋮
The Spasimo di Sicilia Madrid, Prado
This picture was executed for the Church of Sta Maria dello Spasimo in Palermo, where it arrived after a turbulent voyage

132 PL. LVIII

133

136

134 PL. LVII

135

according to Vasari, which involved a shipwreck and a landing at Genoa. In 1622 it was acquired by Philip of Spain, when it was given its present name. Removed to Paris by the French in 1813, it was transferred to canvas; restored to Spain in 1822. On a rock is the inscription RAPHAEL VRBINAS. According to Hartt, the conception can be attributed mainly to Giulio Romano. Unanimously dated 1517, the year which appears in an engraving after this picture by Agostino Veneziano. In a poor state of preservation.

133 🔲⊕ 88×62 1516–18 📋⋮
Holy Family With the Infant St John (Madonna of the Promenade) London, Ellesmere Collection
Once owned by Queen Christina of Sweden and the Duke of Bracciano; it passed to its present location when the Orléans Collection was dispersed in 1792. According to Cavalcaselle, supported by A. Venturi, it was painted by Penni from an idea of Raphael. Gamba assigns the execution to Perino del Vaga. Gronau's date of 1516–8 is generally accepted.

Spandrels from 130 depicting the first ten mythological episodes of Cupid and Psyche. Starting from the top of the first column: Venus and Cupid, Cupid and the Graces, Venus with Ceres and Juno, Venus in her Chariot, Venus and Jove; *second column:* Mercury, Psyche Transported by Cupids, Venus and Psyche, Cupid and Jove, Mercury and Psyche. *(See also Plate LIX).*

134 ⊞ ✪ 40×30 / 1518 ⊟⋮

The Vision of Ezekiel
Florence, Pitti
Mentioned by Vasari in the house of Count Ercolani in Bologna, 'a painting of small figures . . . in the centre a Christ, in the style of Jove, aloft in the sky and around him the four evangelists, as Ezekiel describes them, one in the guise of a man and the other a lion, another, a hawk and (the fourth) an ox ; the countryside below represents the earth, no less rare and beautiful in its smallness than other things in their largeness.' Exhibited in the Uffizi in 1589, the painting was kept in Paris from 1799–1815 by Napoleon ; it then passed to the Pitti. According to Malvasia (*Felsina pittrice*, 1678) eight golden ducats were paid by Ercolani to Raphael in May 1510, which would establish the date of the execution. Nevertheless, Passavant, with the agreement of almost all the more recent critics, believes that this sum was merely a first payment, since the work's stylistic characteristics preclude a dating before 1516, or better 1518. Cavalcaselle assigns the execution to Giulio Romano, but the high quality of the execution, in addition to the originality of the conception, excludes this theory, which is held by some other modern critics. The prophet in ecstasy has been to all intents and purposes eliminated from the picture ; the divine apparition reveals the influence of Michelango. Gamba appropriately imagined the scene projected into the curvature of an apse. The landscape extends into the distance enlarging the space of the foreground. Only the tree in the centre middle ground provides a means of measuring the space.

135 ⊞ ✪ 268×160 / 1518 ⊟⋮

St Michael Subdues Satan
Paris, Louvre
Raphael was commissioned by Lorenzo de' Medici on behalf of Leo X to paint this work, which was sent, together with *The Holy Family* (136), to François I in June 1518. On the edge of the archangel's robe is written : RAPHAEL VRBINAS FACEBAT M.D. XVIII. The various restorations carried out by Primaticcio (1537–40) and Guelin (1685) and the transfer from wood to canvas undertaken by Picault in 1737 have considerably altered the original appearance of the painting. Raphael's contribution must have been limited ; most critics are agreed on Giulio Romano's collaboration ; only Hartt (*Giulio Romano*, 1958) regards this as autograph.

136 ⊞ ✪ 207×140 / 1518 ⊟⋮

Holy Family with St Elizabeth and the Infant St John and Two Angels (The large Holy Family) Paris, Louvre
On the edge of the Virgin's

The central sections of 130. From the top: The Council of the Gods *and* The Marriage Feast.

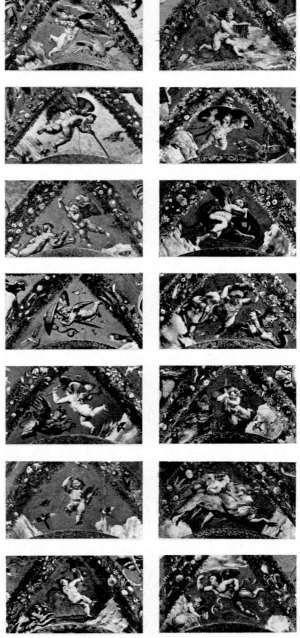

The smaller compartments from 130. From the top of the first column: Cupid and a Hawk, Cupid with a Trident, Cupids with Cerberus, Cupid with Shield and Sword, Cupid with Griffon, Cupid with Wand, Cupid with Panther, Cupid with Shepherd's Pipes, Cupid with Helmet and Shield, Cupid with a Harpy-eagle, Cupid and a Crocodile, Cupid, Lion and Sea Horse, Cupids with a Bow.

117

Study for the child of 136 (Florence, Uffizi).

cloak is the inscription: RAPHAEL VRBINAS / S / PINGEBAT MDXVIII. Sent to François I by Leo X, together with the *St Michael* (see 135); it was restored by Primaticcio and transferred to canvas in 1753. Its poor state of preservation makes attribution difficult. Vasari's biography of Giulio Romano mentions the collaboration of Pippi, which Hartt limits to the figure of St Elizabeth, while assigning the figure of Joseph to Raphael and other parts to Raffaellino del Colle (AB, 1944). The idea for this complex and crowded composition – 'to fill up the illuminated area of the picture' (Ortolani) – can be attributed to Raphael who was searching for unusual effects of colour and lighting which Sebastiano del Piombo criticized in a letter to Michelangelo: 'the figures look smoky, as though made of polished iron.'

137 ▦ ◓ 38 × 32 / 1518-19 ▤ ⋮

Madonna and Child with St Elizabeth and the Infant St John (The small Holy Family) Paris, Louvre
This work was executed for Cardinal Gouffier de Boissy, as was the *Young St John* (128); it subsequently belonged to the Count of Brienne (1622) who sold it to Louis XIV. It was at one time believed to be part of a diptych, together with an allegory of Abundance, bearing the false signature RAPHAEL VRBINAS (Paris, Louvre). A. Venturi assigns this painting to Giulio Romano, executed after Raphael's death. Critics generally regard it as the work of Giulio Romano or Polidoro da Caravaggio from a drawing by Raphael, and date it around 1518–9. A copy in a private French collection was considered by A. Venturi to be closer to the original.

138 ▦ ◓ 178 × 122 / 1518 ▤ ⋮

St Margaret Paris, Louvre
This work may have been painted for Margaret of Navarre. It was restored by Primaticcio at Fontainebleau in 1540 and subsequently badly damaged in a fire (Cassiano dal Pozzo *Diarium*, 1625 Naples, Biblioteca Nazionale). According to Vasari, it was executed by Giulio Romano from drawings of Raphael. It is attributed today to the bottega, and was executed around 1518. The transfer from the panel to canvas caused further damage.

137

138

139

140

141

142 Pl. LXII

139 ▦ ◓ 144 × 110 / 1518 ▤ ⋮

The Holy Family with the Infant St John (Holy Family under the Oak Tree) Madrid, Prado
The building in the left background recalls the Basilica of Maxentius. The landscape on the right has been identified as the valley of the Tiber. It passed to the Prado from the Mediadia of Alcazar in Madrid. Traditionally attributed to Raphael; Cavalcaselle considers it to be by Penni; contemporary opinion tends to assign it to Giulio Romano. It can be dated around 1518. Numerous copies are known.

140 ▦ ◓ 152 × 125 / 1518 ▤ ⋮

Madonna and Child with the Infant St John and St Elizabeth (Madonna of the Divine Love) Naples, Galleria Nazionale di Capodimonte
This *Madonna* may be identified with a work mentioned by Vasari, painted for Lionello da Carpi, lord of Meldola, and subsequently acquired by Cardinal Alessandro Farnese, who left it in 1624 to the Farnese family of Parma. It passed to its present location from the collection of the Bourbons of Naples. There is agreement about the attribution to the school of Raphael.

141 ▦ ◓ 103 × 84 / 1518 ▤ ⋮

The Holy Family with the Infant St John (Madonna of the Rose) Madrid, Prado
This picture came to the Prado from the 'capituolo prioral' of the Escorial. It was largely executed by the bottega, probably by Giulio Romano and Penni, from Raphael's drawings. It can be dated around 1518. Transferred from the panel to canvas; a strip was probably added to the bottom with the foot of Jesus and the rose, which do not appear in the numerous copies.

142 ▦ ◓ 120 × 95 / 1518 ▤ ⋮

Portrait of Joanna of Aragon Paris, Louvre
Commissioned by Bibbiena to send as a gift to François I of France; Alfonso d'Este saw it at Fontainebleau in November 1518. Vasari says that the subject sat for Raphael, who painted the head, but Raphael affirms, when he sent the cartoon to the Duke of Ferrara, that the cartoon was done by an assistant sent expressly to Naples. Cavalcaselle has nevertheless recognized the

hand of Raphael in some of the final retouching. L. Venturi (A, 1926) maintains that the invention can be attributed to Raphael. Restored by Primaticcio and transferred from wood to canvas.

143 ▦ ◓ 99 × 83 / 1518 ▤ ⋮

Portrait of Two Men Paris, Louvre
Traditionally regarded as a portrait of Raphael and his fencing master. The man on the right is most likely to be a pupil of Raphael: Polidoro da Caravaggio, according to Ortolani. It belonged to François I of France; its earlier provenance is unknown. Passavant and Cavalcaselle reject the attribution to Raphael. Waagen, Hourticq (RAAM, 1923), Gombosi (KL, 1933) and Dussler (*Sebastiano del Piombo*, 1942) consider it to be the work of Sebastiano del Piombo. Berenson supports the attribution to Raphael, followed by A. Venturi, Ortolani,

143

Pallucchini (*Sebastian Viniziano*, 1944), Carli, Camesasca and Brizio. The usual date is given as c. 1518.

144 ▦ ◓ 165 × 147 / 1518-19 ▤ ⋮

The Young St John Florence, Galleria dell'Accademia
In the Uffizi by 1589; it subsequently passed to the Pitti and finally to its present location. It has been tentatively identified with the painting which Vasari mentions as having been commissioned for Jacopo da Carpi by Cardinal Colonna. Critics agree in attributing it to Raphael's bottega with a date of 1518–20. There are numerous old copies.

145 ▦ ◓ 154 × 119 / 1518-19 ▤ ⋮

Portrait of Leo X with Cardinals Giulio de' Medici and Luigi de' Rossi Florence, Uffizi
In Vasari's biography of Andrea del Sarto, he relates that

Federico II Gonzaga admired this painting in the house of Ottaviano de' Medici in Florence, and requested it as a gift from Clement VII, who gave his approval and ordered Ottaviano to send it to Gonzaga. Ottaviano, however, according to Vasari, secretly had a copy made by Andrea del Sarto. This account is considered false by C. D'Arco and W. Braghirolli who published (ASA, 1868) some letters from Federico Gonzaga which suggest that by 1525 he had still not received the painting. The fact that it did not leave Florence seems to be confirmed by the commission to execute a copy which was received by Vasari in December 1536. It was placed in the Uffizi in 1589; in 1799 it was removed to France by Napoleon until its return in 1815. A copy attributed to Andrea del Sarto is in Naples. The date of De' Rossi's election to the cardinalship in 1517 and

that of his death in 1519, dates the work to 1518–9. The painting in the Uffizi is generally believed to be by Raphael; Vasari refers to the collaboration of Giulio Romano, which – according to Cavalcaselle – can be seen in the robes and hands of De' Rossi; according to Gamba, in the figure of Giulio de' Medici. The absence of action accentuates rather than diminishes the historical character of this triple portrait.

146 ▦ ◓ 85 × 60 / 1518-19 ▤ ⋮

Portrait of a Young Woman (The Fornarina) Rome, Galleria Nazionale
On the armband is written *Raphael Vrbinas*. Seen by Chancellor Corasduz in 1595 in the house of the Countess of Santafiora, it subsequently belonged to the Buoncompagnis of Rome (in whose possession it is recorded in 1618 by Fabio Chigi in *Commentario alla vita di*

Agostino Chigi) and to the Barberinis (Tezio, *Aedes Barberinae*, 1642). Recently, it was lent to the Galleria Borghese for a short time. The subject was traditionally regarded as the Fornarina, Raphael's mistress, but was identified by Astolfi as the Sienese Margherita Luti, daughter of Francesco, a baker in the quarter of Santa Dorotea in Rome. The traditional attribution to Raphael is sustained by Passavant, Cavalcaselle and Burckhardt; whereas Morelli (1897), followed by Berenson, Seidlitz, Gamba and others, attributed it to Giulio Romano, and dated it after 1520. Those critics favouring the attribution to Raphael include A. Venturi (1935), Ortolani, Gropau, Pittaluga, Camesasca and Brizio. It can be dated 1518–9.

147 ⊞ ✦ 60×40 1518-19 ▤ ⦂
Portrait of a Young Woman
Strasbourg, Musée des Beaux-Arts
Formerly in the Acton Collection in London, it was acquired by Bode in 1890 as a work of Raphael and then passed to its present location. In the 1899 catalogue, it was listed as a work of 'the school of Raphael' (Penni or Giulio Romano); Berenson, Voss and the 1938 catalogue assigned it to Giulio Romano; Fischel mentioned it in 1962 as a work from the school of Raphael. After the removal of nineteenth-century repainting, it appeared in the exhibition in Paris *Le XVIme siècle européen dans les collections publique françaises* as *Raphael?* An X-ray photograph (Laclotte, in the exhibition catalogue) revealed that the hand, the sleeves and the chemise were added at a second stage of the execution. Raphael does not appear to have executed this work which was executed by the bottega around 1518–9. The pose and certain details of the clothing present a remarkable similarity to 121 and 146.

144

148 ⊞ ✦ 74×50 1518-19 ▤ ⦂
Lady with a Veil Hanover, Landesgalerie
Formerly in Bologna, this work passed to the Kestner Collection during the first half of the 19th century; later it was acquired by the Landesgalerie. The traditional attribution to Raphael, accepted doubtfully by Passavant, was rejected by Cavalcaselle, Rosenberg and Gronau. The attribution to Sebastinao del Piombo

145 Pls. LX-LXI

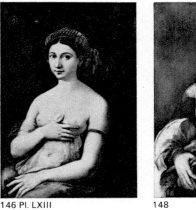

146 Pl. LXIII

148

proposed by Küppers (MFK, 1916), and supported by Gombosi (KL, 1933), was refuted by Dussler (*Sebastiano del Piombo*, 1942) and by Pallucchini (*Sebastian Viniziano*, 1944); A. Venturi and Berenson suggested Giulio Romano, whereas Fischel reaffirmed Raphael's authorship, upheld by the compilers of the Hanover Gallery catalogue (1954), by Longhi, Volpe (PA, 1956) and Camesasca. This attribution has been recently rejected by Brizio, and other critics, who believe it the work of one of Raphael's pupils. The dating proposed by Longhi, 1503–5, instead of the customary dating during Raphael's Roman period, caused much perplexity. It would indeed be difficult to place this work among the Florentine portraits. The restorations carried out in

147

1892, 1930, etc. and the poor state of preservation prevent an accurate opinion.

The Logge

The second series of logge in the building designed by Bramante for Julius II as a façade for the palace of Nicholas III were continued and completed under Leo X by Raphael who also designed the stucco and fresco decorations. The gallery (65 metres long and 4 metres wide) is divided into thirteen cloister-vaulted bays, each frescoed with four scenes with hexagonal, rectangular or curved frames in stucco; the pendentives are decorated with grotesques and architectural motifs attributed to Peruzzi by Lanckoronska (JKS, 1935); on the keystone in the central bay is Leo X's coat of arms; on all the other keystones, figures of victories or putti holding a yoke emblem before he became Pope Leo X. On the first twelve bays are episodes from the Old Testament; the thirteenth episode is taken from the New Testament. The grotesques and stucco decorations extend along the walls and the pilasters. Most of the reliefs illustrate mythological themes, others reproduce famous works, such as the Belvedere *Torso*, Donatello's *St George*,

Lorenzetto's *Jonah* for the Chigi Chapel in Sta Maria del Popolo. Other reliefs illustrate contemporary events of the papal court: *Leo X Blessing a Priest in the Logge*, *The Elephant Annone*, etc. The monochromes on the wainscot return to Biblical themes. Raphael designed the decoration and supervised its execution, in some cases furnishing the drawings. Among the artists working on the execution, as Vasari relates in his life of Raphael, were: Giovanni da Udine, in charge of the decorations, Giulio Romano, Penni, Tommaso Vincidor da Bologna, Vincenzo da San Gimignano, Perino del Vaga, Pellegrino da Modena, Polidoro da Caravaggio, 'and many other painters who supplied various of the scenes and figures and other details that were wanted'. The grotesques can be assigned to Giovanni da Udine and Perino del Vaga; the stucco reliefs are probably the work of Giovanni da Udine who, according to Vasari, rediscovered 'true antique stucco' by mixing powder from the whitest marble available with slaked lime from white travertine. Dollmayr's theory (ASA, 1890), that the decoration of the Logge was begun at the end of 1517, is generally accepted. Fischel and Carli date the work in 1518, while Gamba gives it as 1516. The date 1513, written under one of the stucco victories on the left of the window in the twelfth arcade, cannot be related to the fresco. There is evidence of the completion of

the work in an order of payment dated 11 June, 1519 made to the 'apprentices who painted the loggia' (Archivio Vaticano) and from two letters of the same year announcing the completion: one from Michiel to a Venetian on 4 May, the other from Castiglione to Isabella Gonzaga on 16 June. Clumsy restorations contributed to the decline of the frescoes as well as the inclement weather to which they were exposed until the logge were enclosed with glass in the second half of the 19th century. In 1952 two painted half-pilasters were discovered still intact under a wall built to close in the final arch, which was constructed during the papacy of Paul III (1534–9). These give an idea of the original appearance of the decoration.
The symbols accompanying 149 A (Bay I) apply to all the other paintings in this series pertaining to the Logge.

149 ⊞ ✦ 1518-19 ▤ ⦂
A. Scenes from Genesis
(Bay I)
These episodes illustrate *The Creation of Light*, *The Separation of The Earth from the Water*, *The Creation of the Sun and Moon* and *The Creation of Animals*. the hexagonal-shaped scenes have reticulated frames with figures of angels in the corners, which Fischel attributes to Raphael. The four episodes, attributed to Giulio Romano by Passavant and Cavalcaselle, are considered by most recent critics as the work of Penni from drawings by Giulio Romano, to whom

Detail of the painted grotesques and the stucco reliefs from the wall decorations of 149.

149 A 149 C 149 E 149 G 149 I

149 B 149 D 149 F 149 H 149 J

Hartt, however, attributes the
first scene. According to Gamba,
Raphael commenced the cycle
with *God Separating the Earth
from the Water*. Hartt has
revived a hypothesis put
forward by Cavalcaselle, that
the animals of the fourth scene
were executed from drawings of
Giovanni da Udine, to whom he
assigns all the animals of the
cycle; he also assigns the

landscapes to Polidoro da
Caravaggio. The monochromes
along the base, portraying *God
Sanctifying the Seventh Day*,
were painted – according to
Vasari – together with all the
other monochromes by Perino
del Vaga.
**B. Scenes from the Lives of
Adam and Eve** (Bay II)
*The Creation of Eve, Original
Sin, The Expulsion from Eden,*

and *The Descendants of Seth*.
Cavalcaselle attributes the
first three to Giulio Romano;
most critics today attribute
them to Penni, with the
assistance of Giulio Romano.
The fourth scene is too damaged
to permit an opinion.
Reproductions by Bartoli reveal
that the monochrome on the
base, which was destroyed,
portrayed *Cain and Abel*

*Kneeling before the Altars,
God the Father Facing Abel*, and
Cain Killing Abel.
**C. Scenes from the Life of
Noah** (Bay III)
*The Building of the Ark, The
Flood, The Going Forth from the
Ark* and *The Sacrifice of Noah*.
Vasari assigns the first and
fourth scenes to Giulio Romano;
Cavalcaselle, followed by most
modern critics, considers them

to be by Penni. Cavalcaselle,
supported by Hartt, also regards
the whole of *The Flood* as the
work of Giulio Romano; others
attribute its execution to Penni.
The Going Forth from the Ark is
too damaged to permit reliable
attribution. On the wainscot is
The Rainbow After the Flood.
**D. Scenes from the Lives of
Abraham and Lot** (Bay IV)
Abraham and Melchisedech.

120

149 K

149 M

149 L

The Promise of God, The Meeting with the Angels and *The Flight of Sodom*. The conception of the four stories is generally assigned to Giulio Romano; the execution, to Penni. Hartt, nevertheless, attributes the episodes of *Abraham and the Angels* and *The Flight from Sodom* to Perino del Vaga. The conception of *The Sacrifice of Isaac,*

represented in monochrome on the base, is attributed to Raphael by Cavalcaselle.

E. Scenes from the Life of Isaac (Bay V)
God Appears to Isaac, Abimelech Spies on Isaac and Rebekah, The Benediction of Jacob, and *Esau's Birthright.* Cavalcaselle attributes the first fresco to Giulio Romano. The prevalent tendency today is to recognize the collaboration of Penni in the execution of all four scenes. Hartt, however, assigns the first two to Perino del Vaga because of the elegance of the linear rhythms and the almost feminine grace of the figures. The same scene as the preceding one is represented in monochrome on the base; according to Passavant, the same cartoon was repeated by mistake.

F. Scenes from the Life of Jacob (Bay VI)
Jacob's Dream, The Meeting with Rachel, The Agreement with Laban, The Journey to Canaan. The first scene, traditionally assigned, together with the second, to Pellegrino da Modena, is generally regarded today as the work of Penni. Hartt attributes the scene to Guilio Romano, pointing out the similarity between the figure of Jacob asleep and that of Polyphemus in Villa Madama. Hartt also attributes to Perino del Vaga the other three frescoes, which are usually assigned to Penni (the second and third) and to Giulio Romano (the fourth). The landscapes are assigned to Giovanni da Udine. The monochrome on the base depicts *Jacob's Struggle with the Angel.*

G. Scenes from the Life of Joseph (Bay VII)
The Interpretation of the Dreams to the Brothers, Joseph Sold into Egypt, The Temptation by Potiphar's Wife, The

Interpretation of Pharaoh's Dreams. The conception of these four stories is usually assigned to Giulio Romano; the execution to Penni; the landscapes to Giovanni da Udine. Hartt proposes the authorship of Perino del Vaga for the first two scenes and that of Giulio Romano for the third, relating it to the *Adonis Fleeing from Mars* in the Hall of Psyche in Palazzo Te in Mantua. The monochrome on the base represents *Joseph Identifying Himself to his Brothers.*

H. Scenes from the Life of Moses (Bay VIII)
Moses Rescued from the Nile, The Burning Bush, The Crossing of The Red Sea, Moses Striking the Rock. All but the third scene are generally attributed to Giulio Romano, probably with the collaboration of Penni. Different views exist, however, concerning the third scene, which A. Venturi and some modern critics assign to Giulio Romano, while Cavalcaselle, supported by certain recent studies, credits Perino del Vaga. The monochrome on the base represents *The Manna From Heaven.*

I. Scenes from the Lives of Moses and Joshua (Bay IX)
The Giving of the Ten Commandments, The Worship of the Golden Calf, The Column of Smoke, The Presentation of the Ten Commandments to the Hebrews. The four frescoes were attributed by Taja (*Descrizione del Vaticano,* 1750) to Raffaellino del Colle, who was not, however, mentioned by Vasari among the artists working on the Logge. Today they are attributed to Giulio Romano, probably with the assistance of Penni. The monochrome on the base is possibly *Joshua Haranguing the People of Israel* (Passavant)

J. Scenes from the Life of Joshua (Bay X)
The Passage of the Jordan, The Fall of Jericho, The Sun and the Moon Stand Still, The Land is Divided by Lot. Vasari assigned the first and third stories to Perino del Vaga; this attribution is generally accepted and extended to the two others. Cavalcaselle maintained that Giulio Romano planned *The Sun and the Moon,* pointing out that Passavant saw the cartoon in the house of Gaddi in Florence. An engaraving by Bartoli, which is supposed to reproduce the corresponding monochrome, shows two standing figures and a passageway on each side of a door; but Cavalcaselle notes that the monochrome 'could never have been situated there since there is actually a door at that point opening onto the old Hall of the Grooms.'

K. Scenes from the Life of David (Bay XI)
The Consecration, The Encounter with Goliath, The Victory over the Assyrians, Bathsheba's Toilet. Unanimously attributed to Perino del Vaga, who might have worked from drawings of Penni (for the first and fourth scenes), and to Giulio Romano

(for the second and third). The subject of the monochrome decorating the base is unknown.

L. Scenes from the Life of Solomon (Bay XII)
The Consecration, The Judgment, The Meeting with the Queen of Sheba, The Building of Solomon's Temple. The four frescoes are generally assigned to Perino del Vaga, but Cavalcaselle attributed the first two and the fourth to Giulio Romano.

M. Scenes from the Life of Christ (Bay XIII)
The Nativity, The Epiphany, The Baptism, The Last Supper. Vasari attributed these scenes to Perino del Vaga (but he does not mention The Epiphany), an opinion shared by later critics. Filippini (BDA, 1929) attributed them, however, to Tommaso Vincidor da Bologna, on the basis of comparisons between the Nativity and the tapestry of the same subject from the second Vatican series. According to Hartt, the frescoes represent the combined efforts of Penni and Giulio Romano. *The Resurrection* is illustrated in monochrome on the base.

---

150 ⊞ ⊕   1518-19   ▤ ⁰⁰

The First Loggia Rome, The Vatican
On 4 May, 1519, Michiel wrote a letter from Rome about Raphael's work in the Vatican: 'Raphael of Urbino has painted four rooms in the Vatican (the Stanze) for the Pope, and a very long loggia (the Logge) and

went straight on to paint two others (logge) which will be of exceptional beauty.' The 'very long loggia' is the Logge (149) decorated with Biblical themes – 'Raphael's Bible' – and one of the 'others' is the Loggetta (151); the reference to the other loggia is probably to the extremely fine decorations in the first order of logge, repainted by Alessandro Mantovani in the second half of the 19th century. In Michiel's diaries a note dated 27 December, 1519 reads: 'during the past few days the lower of the three loggias in the Palace, on the side facing Rome, was finished; it was most vulgarly painted with foliage, grotesques and other similar fantasies which cost little but looked ostentatious. But in the loggia above immediately adjoining are paintings of great merit and charm which were designed by Raphael.' From these remarks we may conclude that Raphael left all of the decoration of the lower loggia to his bottega.

151 ⊞ ⊕   1519   ▤ ⦂

The Loggetta Rome, The Vatican
In Michiel's letter, quoted above (150), listing the frescoes done by Raphael in the Vatican, one of the '... two other logge which will be of exceptional beauty,' would seem to refer to the loggia on the ground floor which was repainted by Alessandro Mantovani during the second half of the 19th century; the other one cannot be the third-floor loggia painted by Giovanni da Udine after 1550, and is consequently usually identified as the rectangular

Partial view of the Loggetta on the third floor of the Vatican (151).

room (15.74 metres × 3.12 and 4.64 metres high from the centre of the vaulted ceiling) known as the Loggetta, located next to the third loggia and near the Stufetta of Cardinal Bibbiena. On one side of the Loggetta three large archways, alternating with four smaller ones, open onto the Cortile del Maresciallo. On the opposite wall three arched compartments, adorned with grotesques, correspond to the large archways ; mythological scenes painted on a black ground decorate the lunettes : *Apollo and Olympus, Apollo and Marsyas* and a third scene, which is lost, portraying (according to De Campos) *The Flaying of Marsyas.* Opposite the smaller openings are *trompe l'oeil* niches, containing statues representing the seasons, flanked by small columns supporting a false opening and four niches. Of these niches only three remain, the fourth having been destroyed to allow for a door (De Campos). Above the niches are scenes of single figures or groups of figures ; the lunettes

152

at each end of the loggia portray a group of *Dancers* and *Vulcan's Forge.* Well-known statues and animals, framed with architectural and plant motifs, complete the decoration of the walls and ceiling. Scenes of mythological and historical episodes alternate with geometric figures along the base. Raphael's design for the decorations was carried out under his supervision by Giulio Romano, Penni, Perino del

Vaga, Giovanni da Udine and other lesser-known assistants. The dating of the cycle is generally based on Michiel's reference which sets the execution at 1519 ; Hartt proposes 1516. Parts of the decoration were discovered under a later layer of plaster in 1906. Steinmann (K, 1905–6 and MK, 1906) identified the discovery as the aviary which Julius II first commissioned Peruzzi and then Raphael to paint. The cycle was restored from 1943–6 ; the parts that could be put back into place were blended in with lighter tones and are therefore easily recognizable.

152 🔲 ⊘ 200 × 145 / 1519 📄 ⋮
The Visitation Madrid, Prado
In the foreground is the meeting of Mary and Elizabeth ; in the left background is the Baptism

153 Pl. LXIV

Lunette depicting Vulcan's forge with Cupids and Grotesques *(151).*

Apollo and Olympus ; *one of the three scenes against a black ground (151)*

One of the Seasons; one figure in the grotesques of 151

of Christ. Below is written : RAPHAEL VRBINAS F. MARINVS. BRANCONIVS F. F. Marino Branconio commissioned the painting for the Church of S. Silvestro in Aquila. It passed to the Escorial in 1655 ; transferred to Paris in 1813 during the Napoleonic regime and was restored in 1822. Raphael's conception was worked up by his bottega ; the execution could be by Penni, Giulio Romano or Perino del Vaga. It can be dated around 1519.

153 🔲 ⊘ 405 × 278 / 1518 - 20 📄 ⋮
The Transfiguration Rome, Pinacoteca Vaticana
The commission for the Cathedral of Narbonne was allotted to Raphael in 1517 by Cardinal Giulio de' Medici, Bishop of Narbonne. In 1523 the painting was placed in S. Pietro in Montorio in Rome where it remained until 1797 when it was removed to France ; restored in 1815, it passed to its present location. According to tradition, which is partially confirmed by reports of that period (see pp. 83 and 84, 1517 and 1518), Raphael

received the commission in competition with Sebastiano del Piombo who executed *The Raising of Lazarus.* It is not certain how far the execution had proceeded at the time of Raphael's death. Most critics believe that most of the panel, including the lower half, was painted by Raphael. A few details were completed by his pupils between 1520–2. There is a request for payment made by Castiglione on behalf of Giulio Romano on 7 May, 1522, to Cardinal Giulio de' Medici ('Giulio, pupil of R. of Urbino, is the creditor of a certain sum of money for the panel which the aforementioned R did for Your most Illustrious Eminence') and a document from the monastery of Sta Maria Novella in Florence which attests to a debt of 220 ducats owed to Pippi 'for the altar piece painted by Master R. of Urbino.' Vogel (MKF, 1920) rightly maintains, however, that the payments were made to Giulio Romano as Raphael's heir and not as his assistant. The documents do not establish for certain whether *The Transfiguration* was finished before Raphael's death. Vasari states that 'Raphael worked continually (on the painting) achieving the ultimate perfection.' Sebastiano del Piombo reinforces this testimony with his letter of 12 April, 1520, six days after Raphael's death, to Michelangelo : 'I believe you know how that poor fellow Raphael of Urbino died . . . and I tell you that today I brought my panel once again to the Vatican with the one by Raphael and I was not ashamed.' Assistants collaborated to a limited extent on the lower half, but the invention is undoubtedly Raphael's. As Bertini points out, the unity of the work is created by directing the gestures of the figures in the lower half of the composition towards the figure

Studies for 153: St Andrew, in the foreground and the two figures in the centre, middle ground (London, British Museum; Paris, Louvre; Oxford, Ashmolean Museum).

Geometrical study after the group in the upper half of 153 (London, British Museum).

of Christ. The development of the painting towards its final scheme can be traced through the preparatory drawings, which are analyzed in detail by Oberhuber (JBM, 1962). Initially, the scene with the possessed boy was omitted, and Christ was standing on the ground. At the intermediary stage there are the two scenes, but Christ is still on the ground.

The many detailed studies, sketches, and highly finished auxiliary cartoons reveal Raphael's careful preparation of the finished work. Christ rises in a halo of light between Moses and Elijah, in the presence of Peter, James and John ; below, the possessed boy is led to the apostles to be cured. The two episodes are recounted together in the Bible (*Matthew*, XVII 1–20) as well. The martyrs Felicissimus and Agapitus kneel above on the left ; the saints' day in their name was celebrated on 6 August, the same day as that devoted to the celebration of the Transfiguration. It is likely, as Mellini suggests, (CDA, 1962), that their presence had a precise liturgical significance related to the daily mass. The dramatic character of the painting, which was immensely popular during the 16th and 17th centuries, is primarily due to the light which comes from two sources and to the contrast of the two scenes. The upper half is a solemn and symmetrical composition, like a mosaic or a bas-relief for a sarcophagus ; the lower half is a

tumultuous alternation of violent light and shadow, with strongly dramatic gestures and an intense, Leonardesque rendering of expression. The novelty and originality of the composition, with its powerfully theatrical content and wealth of themes, was to provide inspiration for such differing artists as Annibale Carracci, Guido Reni, Poussin, Caravaggio and Rubens.

The Sala di Costantino

Vasari relates in his biographies of Raphael and Penni that Raphael was commissioned by Leo X in 1517 to decorate the fourth Stanza of the Vatican, which was completed after Raphael's death by his pupils. Further information, supplied in the biography of Giulio Romano, states that Raphael executed the cartoons and ordered the preparation of one of the walls for oil paint. On 12 April, 1520, six days after Raphael's death, Sebastiano del Piombo wrote to Michelangelo in Florence requesting Michelangelo to obtain for him through Cardinal Giulio de' Medici the commission to decorate the Sala. Michelangelo probably secured a portion of the work for his friend, but on 6 September, Sebastiano wrote again to Michelangelo complaining that the job had been taken away from him because Raphael's apprentices had the Master's drawings for the Constantine episodes. On 15 December, 1520, Leonardo

Sellaio informed Michelangelo that the pope was preparing to visit the Sala and that the paintings which had already been executed were 'coarse.' A different opinion was expressed by Castiglione a year later (16 December, 1521), when he wrote to Federigo Gonzaga that he considered the decoration of the room, which was half completed, admirable. These and other reports have been variously interpreted by recent studies. It seems nevertheless certain that with the exception of *The Battle of*

tne Milvian Bridge, Raphael's contribution was limited to planning the decoration and that the execution and the composition of the remaining paintings was carried out by his pupils after Raphael's death. The historical and political themes of the second and third Stanze reach their fulfilment in the Sala. The main frescoes, which are painted like wall tapestries, represent *The Baptism of Constantine*, *The Vision of the Cross*, *The Battle of*

the Milvian Bridge and *The Presentation of Rome to the Pope*. At the sides are niches containing images of popes flanked by angels and allegorical figures, two of which, Justice and Forebearance (154 E and F), are painted in oil. Along the simulated marble wainscot, caryatids surmounting the Medici coat of arms alternate with *trompe l'oeil* bronze bas-reliefs of scenes from the life of Constantine painted in monochrome. Perino del Vaga painted the spandrels of the windows with allegorical

motifs and historical subjects : *Converted Pagans Destroying their Idols, St Silvester Chains the Dragon, Constantine Returns from Jerusalem with his Mother, St Gregory Prepares a Sermon*. The work was completed under Clement VII before Giulio Romano's departure for Mantua by September 1524. In 1585 the beamed ceiling of the room was replaced by a false vaulted one which seriously distorted the effect of the decoration.

A. The Vision of the Cross

The idea for this composition, as well as certain details, was inspired by the *Adlocutio* motif represented in more than one place on Trajan's Column. On the block from which Constantine addresses his soldiers before the battle against Maxentius, is written : ADLOCUTIO QUA DIVINITATIS IMPULSI CONSTANTINIANI VICTORIAM REPERERE. A cross in the sky bears an

inscription in Greek : 'With this sign you will conquer.' According to Taja (*Descrizione del . . . Vaticano*, 1750), the dwarf in the right foreground resembles Gradasso Berettai, the jester of Cardinal Ippolito de' Medici ; in the background, beyond the Tiber, the mausoleums of Hadrian and Augustus can be seen. From Vasari on the fresco has been attributed to Giulio Romano. Hartt, who considers the execution of inferior quality, proposes the extensive collaboration of Raffaellino del Colle based on cartoons of Romano who supposedly contributed the figure of the dwarf. The monochromes below represent *Constantine's Army Nearing Rome* (the larger one) and *The Entry into Rome* (the two smaller ones).

154 田 ✣ 1520-24 目:

B. The Battle of the Milvian Bridge

This work contains many echoes of ancient Roman sculpture. The figure of Constantine is taken from the bas-relief on the Arch of Constantine. Above, on the left, is a structure probably representing Villa Madama, then under construction from plans of Raphael. According to Passavant and Cavalcaselle, Giulio Romano painted the

154 B

154 A

154 D

154C

154 E

154 F

155

fresco after preparing the cartoon under Raphael's supervision. On the other hand a sixteenth-century biographer Paolo Giovio, who had known Raphael, writes that the fresco was *completed* by pupils. The drawing in the Ashmolean at Oxford (Parker, No. 569) is further evidence that the design was Raphael's.

 **154** 1520-24

C. The Baptism of Constantine

The baptism takes place in a temple that closely resembles the Lateran Baptistry ; Pope Silvester has the features of Clement VII. On the book held by the priest is written : 'Hodie salus Urbi et Imperio facta est ;' in the left and right foregrounds respectively are the inscriptions : 'LAVACRUM RENASCENTIS VITAE C. VAL. CONSTANTINI' and 'CLEMENS VII PONT. MAX. A LEONE X COEPTUM CONSUMAVIT MDXXIIII.' The execution is customarily attributed to Penni with some collaboration by Giulio Romano, to whom Hartt assigns the architecture.

154 1520-24

D. The Presentation of Rome

Disregarding Valla's demonstration that the Donation of Constantine was a forgery, the Medici popes ordered the completion of this episode. In a temple reminiscent of the old St Peter's, Constantine offers Pope Silvester (a portrait of Clement VII) a statue of the goddess of Rome, symbolizing temporal sovereignty. Vasari identified portraits of Giulio Romano, Castiglione, Pontano, Marullo and others in the fresco. Passavant and Cavalcaselle,

supported by almost all subsequent studies, attributed the fresco to Giulio Romano with the possible collaboration of Raffaellino del Colle and Penni (Hartt) for the background figures.

 **154** 1520

E. Justice

An oil painting of the allegorical figure next to the effigy of Urban I. Cavalcaselle believed in the participation of Raphael. Gamba attributes the entire execution to Raphael, a theory which is not generally accepted. In a letter dated 3 July, 1520, Sebastiano del Piombo seems to refer to the figures as the work of Raphael's apprentices. Raphael probably intended that the walls of the entire room should be done in oil, but Vasari relates that because of the poor results of the first attempts, or because of a preference for the more rapid, traditional process of frescoing, the apprentices 'pulled down the whole outer layer which had been prepared for oil paint,' sparing only the figures already painted. Vasari's story suggests that Raphael was responsible for the design of this part of the decoration.

156

154 1520

F. Forebearance

An oil painting of the allegorical figure next to the effigy of Clement I. Cavalcaselle attributes the execution to Giulio Romano and Penni despite its strong Raphaelesque characteristics. Today it is almost unanimously attributed to Giulio Romano. A considerable darkening of the colours has been noted.

155 144×115 1522-23

The Holy Family with the Infant St John and St Elizabeth ('La Perla') Madrid, Prado

In the foreground are the Virgin and Child, St Joseph and St Elizabeth ; in the left background, Joseph among classical-style ruins ; on the right, a Roman countryside. Reumont (ASRP, 1881) believed that this is *The Nativity of Our Lord* which, according to Vasari, was executed by Raphael for the counts of Canossa, who sold it to Cardinal Luigi d'Este ; the cardinal gave it to Caterina Nobili Sforza, Countess of Santafiora, who in turn sold it to Vincenzo I Gonzaga for fifty scudi. This could be the *Madonna* which Vincenzo I acquired from the Canossas in 1604 in exchange for the fief of Cagliano in Monferrato. The painting was subsequently sold to Charles I of England in 1627 and then passed to the collection of Philip IV of Spain, who called it 'the pearl' of his collections. Taken to Paris in 1813 by Napoleon, it was restored to Spain two years later. From Cavalcaselle on, the execution has been attributed to Giulio Romano with the date 1518, yet Hartt makes a convincing case for Giulio Romano's authorship of the work, undertaken after Raphael's death between 1522-3.

156 354×230 1524-25

The Coronation of the Virgin and the Apostles at Her Tomb (The Monteluce Coronation) Rome, Pinacoteca Vaticana

Commissioned about 1501-3 by the nuns of Monteluce, it was executed by Giulio Romano and Penni after Raphael's death and was kept in Paris from 1797–1815 by Napoleon. The composition is divided horizontally by the clouds into two parts, of which the upper one was executed by Giulio Romano and the lower one, by Penni. It is likely, as Passavant suggests, that Giulio Romano made use of preparatory drawings by Raphael. J. Shearman argues that there is a fundamental difference in the nature of the finished painting and that which Raphael had contracted to supply. He suggests that the present picture is two paintings joined, and that the bottom half belongs to the *Assunta* projected for the Chigi Chapel in Sta Maria del Popolo (JWCI, 1961). The predella is by Berto di Giovanni.

Other works mentioned in the early sources

In addition to those works which could be included in the chronological sequence of the catalogue, there are some works, listed below, which are attributed to Raphael in the early sources, but which cannot be dated precisely. Many works are listed in the early sources ; only those with plausible attributions to Raphael are mentioned here.

Portrait of Tebaldeo

This work, mentioned in a letter from Bembo to Bibbiena on 19 April, 1516, cannot be identified with the Budapest Gentleman (see 120) attributed to Sebastiano del Piombo, nor with the presumed 'portrait of Tebaldeo' in the museum at Naples. According to Gamba, a portrait in the Uffizi, which is believed to be a portrait of the poet, could be a copy of the now lost original by Raphael.

Triumph of Bacchus

Numerous letters refer to this picture, which Raphael was commissioned to paint in 1517 for Alfonso I d'Este and which was left unfinished on Raphael's death. There is no trace of it after 1520 (see *Outline Biography*).

Portrait of Lorenzo de Medici

Mentioned in several letters from Lorenzo (22 January and 4 February 1518), it was seen by Vasari in the house of Ottaviano de' Medici's heirs in Florence. Various copies are known, none of which is attributable to Raphael (Montpellier, Florence, Colworth).

Copy of Lorenzo de' Medici (Montpellier, Musée Fabre).

Portrait of Baldassar Castiglione

In a letter to Alfonso I d'Este, sent from Rome on 12 September, 1519, the envoy Paulucci of Ferrara relates that he was not received by Raphael, who was engaged in painting Castiglione's portrait. This must refer to a second portrait of Castiglione (see 114) and has been identified with a painting formerly in the collection of Cardinal Valenti Gonzaga, later in the Torlonia gallery and finally in the Galleria

Nazionale Rome ; this is definitely not by Raphael (GNI, 1896). According to A. Venturi (A, 1918), Raphael invented an excuse in order not to receive Paulucci.

Madonna

A *Madonna 'manu Raphaelis'* was left to Castiglione by Cardinal Bibbiena in his will (8 November, 1520).

The Annunciation

An *Annunciation* by Raphael was sent by De Grassis from Rome to Bologna to be copied by Francia. There is no information as to what happened to the original or the copy ; nevertheless, Gualandi (*Nuova raccolta di lettere sulla pittura*, 1844) published a letter sent to Rome on 22 January, 1583, by Cardinal Delfina to the Grand Duchess Bianca of Tuscany, announcing that an *Annunciation* by Raphael had been sent.

Portrait of a 'Parmesan'

Mentioned by Michiel in 1530 in the house of Antonio Foscarini in Venice ; '(half-length) portrait in oil on wood, showing a Parmesan who was favourite of Pope Julius, painted by Raphael of Urbino for the Bishop of Lodi.'

St Jerome

This work is mentioned by Michiel in the house of Marco Mantova Benavides in Padua, c. 1530.

Portrait of Beatrice Ferrarese

This portrait is mentioned by Vasari. According to Milanesi (*Commento alle Vite del Vasari*, III), the Beatrice in question was a courtesan of Rome and the portrait was painted for Lorenzo de Medici, Duke of Urbino. Milanesi also mentions a letter from Beatrice Ferrarese to the duke on 23 April, 1517 (Florence, Archivio di Stato).

St Agatha

Mentioned by Goethe and in certain inventories in Bologna. Filippini (CDA, 1925) proposed identifying the work with the London St Catherine (84), but received no critical support.

Portrait of Bishop Carondolet

A portrait of 'Charondolet' is mentioned in an anonymous biography of Raphael published by Comoli (Rome, 1791), which proposes to identify the subject as Giovanni Carondolet, Bishop of Besançon. A work in the Thyssen-Bormemisza Collection in Lugano, portraying the Archbishop of Bitonto, Ferry Carondolet, dictating to Guicciardini, was formerly assigned to the school of Raphael by Passavant who saw it in the collection of the dukes of Grafton in Euston Hall ; Cavalcaselle believed that it might be by Lotto. It is today almost unanimously attributed to Sebastiano del Piombo.

Appendix: Raphael's other artistic activities

Modern criticism has pointed out that a comprehensive study of Raphael must include his architectural works. Vasari's life of Raphael begins with the heading: 'painter and architect.' The fundamental buildings for this side of Raphael's activities are the Chigi Chapel and Villa Madama in Rome (see *Outline Biography*); in other cases, buildings wholly or partially planned by him have undergone radical alterations. S. Eligio degli Orefici and St Peter's in Rome; or we have only indirect reports of his work: Palazzo Branconio dell'Aquila, Rome, or unverified attributions: Palazzo Pandolfi in Florence and Palazzo Caffarelli in Rome. Even such limited information allows us to trace Raphael's development as an architect from his direct dependence upon Bramante to his development of a new style which was to change the course of architecture in Italy and abroad. Raphael also undertook some sculpture, more from a dilletante's point of view than a strictly professional one (see *Outline Biography*, 1516). He was much sought after for countless important commissions; he also engaged in lesser projects, and made designs for goldsmiths and mantelpieces, etc. With M.A.Raimondi, he successfully produced prints from his drawings. This remained an example, from the commercial as well as the artistic point of view, for artists through the centuries. Having already referred to Raphael's writings in defence of the classical remains in Rome and his archaeological and scholarly interests (which even took the form of commissions to literati and other experts for the translation of ancient texts and for archaeological activities), we have only to mention Raphael's modest attempts at poetry. Five of Raphael's sonnets (see R. Sanzio, *Tutti gli scritti*, Milan (B.U.R.) 1956.)

(Above) The Chigi Chapel in Sta Maria del Popolo in Rome (1515 c.) echoing Bramante's concepts for St Peter's. (Left) Statue of Jonah *in the Chigi Chapel, carved by Lorenzetto from drawings by Raphael, who may have helped with the execution.*

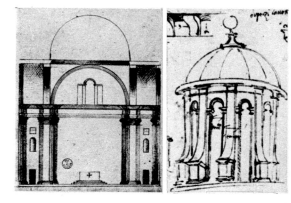

(Above, left) Complete elevation and partial sketch of the lantern of S. Eligio degli Orefici in Rome (1513 c., Florence, Uffizi). – (Left) Drawing, possibly by Parmigianino (ibid.) reproducing the façade of Palazzo Branconio dell'Aquila in Rome, pulled down in the 17th century to make room for Bernini's colonnade for St Peter's.

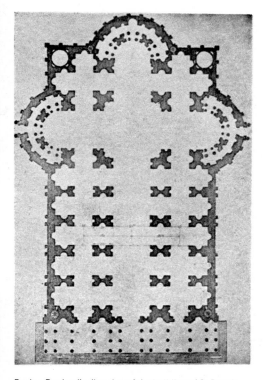

During Raphael's direction of the building of St Peter's, he proposed the transformation of the Greek-cross plan to a basilican one, as documented by this plate after Raphael's design, published in Sebastiano Serlio's Trattato. *(Below) First draft (detail) for a plate in precious metal; 1510 c. (Windsor, Royal Library).*

(Above, left and centre) Exterior and interior view of the loggia of Villa Madama on the slopes of Monte Mario in Rome, designed after 1516. The development of the Italian garden was greatly influenced by this building, with its attractive setting and the richness of the decoration, which represented a departure from the principles of Bramante.

(Left) The Slaughter of the Innocents, print by M. A. Raimondi from drawings by Raphael (1510 c.). Another celebrated work of the same genre is The Judgment of Paris, *which provided inspiration for paintings and sculpture of Italian and French mannerists, Rubens and later artists up to Manet and Renoir.*

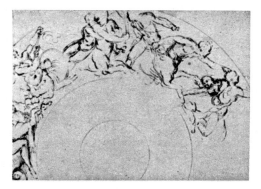

Index

Thematic Index

This index refers to subjects of Raphael's art as set out in the present work. The numbers refer to the items in the Catalogue.

127